WITHDRAWN

Contents

A Message From USA Volleyball

As the national governing body of a sport that has 46 million participants in the United States and an estimated 800 million players worldwide, USA Volleyball considers coaching of paramount importance to everyone involved with the future of the game. Our mission is to develop the sport of volleyball. The best way to harness the potential of the sport's astonishing popularity is through effective and inspirational coaching.

With more than 100,000 members registered through 29 member organizations in 35 regions of the United States, USA Volleyball has the perfect network in place to make an impact on the country's volleyball players—and coaches. For this reason, eight years ago the Coaching Accreditation Program (CAP) was formed to help foster consistency in coaching techniques. CAP promotes the principles practiced by the most effective coaches in the world. The sequential format of the program allows coaches, on any level, to develop their talents continually as they ascend through course levels. The Level I course can provide a solid base from which to begin your coaching career, and you need not feel pressured to continue through all five levels available in CAP.

In addition to the CAP program, USA Volleyball has embarked on a joint venture with the American Volleyball Coaches Association (AVCA) to form an entity called Volleyball Informational Products (VIP), which is dedicated to providing educational resources for coaches through the most up-to-date multimedia productions available.

Indeed, USA Volleyball shows its commitment to excellence in promoting coaching publications such as the American Sport Education Program's *Coaching Youth Volleyball*. This resource strengthens our educational outreach.

It takes a special individual to teach, whether the subject is the cell membrane in biochemistry or a jump serve in volleyball. The same character traits that make good teachers also motivate good learners. USA Volleyball and the AVCA commend every reader of this book for caring to learn and for the dedication you possess to becoming a better coach. We will continue to assist you in all your educational endeavors in volleyball.

Welcome to Coaching!

Coaching young people is an exciting way to be involved in sport. But it isn't easy. The untrained coach may be overwhelmed by the responsibilities involved in helping athletes through their early sport experiences. Preparing youngsters physically and mentally in their sport and providing them with a positive role model are among the difficult—but rewarding—tasks you will assume as a coach.

This book will help you meet the challenges and experience the rewards of coaching young athletes. We call it *Coaching Youth Volleyball* because it is intended for coaches who are working with developing volleyball players. In this book you'll learn how to apply general coaching principles and teach volleyball rules, skills, and strategies successfully to kids. This book also serves as a text for the American Sport Education Program's (ASEP) Rookie Coaches Course.

We hope you will find coaching rewarding and that you will continue to learn more about coaching and your sport so that you can be the best possible coach for your young athletes.

If you would like more information about ASEP and its Rookie Coaches Course, please contact us at

ASEP
P.O. Box 5076
Champaign, IL 61825-5076
(800) 747-5698

Good Coaching!

Unit 1

Who, Me . . . a Coach?

If you are like most youth league coaches, you have probably been recruited from the ranks of concerned parents, sport enthusiasts, or community volunteers. And, like many rookie and veteran coaches, you probably have had little formal instruction on how to coach. But when the call went out for coaches to assist with the local youth volleyball program, you answered because you like children and enjoy volleyball, and perhaps because you want to be involved in a worthwhile community activity.

I Want to Help, but . . .

Your initial coaching assignment may be difficult. Like many volunteers, you may not know everything there is to know about volleyball or about how to work with children between the ages of 6 and 14. Relax, because *Coaching Youth Volleyball* will help you learn the basics of coaching volleyball effectively. In the coming pages you will find the answers to such common questions as these:

- What do I need to be a good coach?
- How can I best communicate with my players?
- How do I go about teaching sport skills?
- What can I do to promote safety?
- What should I do when someone is injured?
- What are the basic rules, skills, and strategies of volleyball?
- What practice drills will improve my players' volleyball skills?

Before answering these questions, let's take a look at what's involved in being a coach.

Am I a Parent or a Coach?

Many coaches are parents, but the two roles should not be confused. Unlike your role as a parent, as a coach you are responsible not only to yourself and your child, but also to the organization, all the players on the team (including your child), and their parents. Because of this additional responsibility, your behavior on the volleyball court will be different from your behavior at home, and your son or daughter may not understand why.

For example, imagine the confusion of a young boy who is the center of his parents' attention at home but is barely noticed by his father/coach in the sport setting. Or consider the mixed signals received by a young girl whose volleyball skill is continually evaluated by a mother/coach who otherwise rarely comments on her daughter's activities. You need to explain to your son or daughter your new responsibilities and how they will affect your relationship when coaching.

Take the following steps to avoid such problems in coaching your child:

- Ask your child if he or she wants you to coach the team.
- Explain why you wish to be involved with the team.
- Discuss how your interactions will change when you take on the role of coach at practices or games.
- Limit your coach behavior to when you are in the coaching role.

- Avoid parenting during practice or game situations, to keep your role clear in your child's mind.
- Reaffirm your love for your child, irrespective of his or her performance on the volleyball court.

What Are My Responsibilities as a Coach?

A coach assumes the responsibility of doing everything possible to ensure that the youngsters on his or her team will have an enjoyable and safe sporting experience while they learn sport skills.

Provide an Enjoyable Experience

Volleyball should be fun. Even if nothing else is accomplished, make certain your players have fun. Take the fun out of volleyball and you'll take the kids out of sport.

Children enter sport for a number of reasons (e.g., to meet and play with other children, to develop physically, and to learn skills), but their major objective is to have fun. Help them satisfy this goal by injecting humor and variety into your practices. Also, make games nonthreatening, festive experiences for your players. Such an approach will increase your players' desire to participate in the future, which should be the biggest goal of youth sport. Unit 2 will help you learn how to satisfy your players' yearning for fun and keep winning in perspective. And unit 3 will describe how you can effectively communicate this perspective to them.

Provide a Safe Experience

If one thing keeps kids out of volleyball, it's the belief that volleyball is only for older, more mature athletes. "Kids can't hit a ball over that high net" is a common excuse for introducing volleyball only after kids have reached their teens. But volleyball can be adapted to be the perfect game for kids. Children and their parents should be reassured that you can make participation in youth volleyball fun and safe, even for seven-year-olds.

You are responsible for planning and teaching activities in such a way that the progression between activities minimizes risks (see units 4 and 5). Further, you must ensure that the facility at which your team practices and plays and the equipment that team members use are free of hazards. Finally, you need to protect yourself from any legal liability that might arise from your involvement as a coach. Unit 5 will help you take the appropriate precautions.

Provide Opportunities for Children With Disabilities

There's a possibility that a child with a disability of some kind will register for your team. Don't panic! Your youth sport administrator or a number of organizations (see appendix A) can provide you with information to help you best meet this child's needs.

As a coach, you need to know about the Americans with Disabilities Act (ADA). Passed in 1990, the ADA gives individuals the same legal protection against discrimination on such bases as disabilities as is provided against discrimination on the basis of race, gender, and class. The law does recognize that there are times when including a player with a disability might risk the safety of that individual and other players, but no clear legal precedents have been established. In general, the law requires that "reasonable accommodations" be made to include children with disabilities into

organized sport programs. If a parent or child approaches you on the subject, and you aren't sure what to do, talk to the director in charge of your volleyball program. If you make any decision on your own pertaining to the ADA, you may be vulnerable to a lawsuit.

Keep in mind that these children want to participate alongside their able-bodied peers. Give them the same support and encouragement that you give other athletes, and model their inclusion and acceptance for all your athletes.

Teach Basic Volleyball Skills

In becoming a coach, you take on the role of educator. You must teach your players the fundamental skills and strategies necessary for success in volleyball. That means that you need to "go to school."

If you don't know the basics of volleyball now, you can learn them by reading the second half of this book, units 6, 7, and 8. But even if you know volleyball as a player, do you know how to teach it? This book will help you get started. There are also many helpful volleyball books on the market, including those offered by Human Kinetics. See the information in the back of this book or call (800) 747-4457 for more information.

You'll also find it easier to provide good educational experiences for your players if you plan your practices. Unit 4 of this manual provides some guidelines for the planning process.

Getting Help

Veteran coaches in your league are an especially good source of help for you. They have all experienced the same emotions and concerns you are facing, and their advice can be invaluable as you work through your first season.

You can get additional help by watching volleyball coaches in practices and games, attending workshops, reading volleyball publications, and studying instructional videos. In addition to the American Sport Education Program (ASEP), USA Volleyball will assist you in obtaining more volleyball coaching information.

USA Volleyball
3595 E. Fountain Blvd., Suite I-2
Colorado Springs, CO 80910-1740
(800) 275-8782

Coaching volleyball is a rewarding experience. And your players will be rewarded if you learn all you can about coaching so you can be the best volleyball coach you can be.

Unit 2

What Tools Do I Need as a Coach?

Have you purchased the traditional coaching tools—things like whistles, coaching clothes, court shoes, and a clipboard? They'll help you coach, but to be a successful coach you'll need five other tools that cannot be bought. These tools are available only through self-examination and hard work; they're easy to remember with the acronym COACH:

C—Comprehension

O—Outlook

A—Affection

C—Character

H—Humor

Comprehension

Comprehension of the rules, skills, and tactics of volleyball is required. It is essential that you understand the basic elements of the sport. To help you learn about the game, units 6-8 describe rules, skills, and tactics and include a variety of drills to use in developing young players' skills.

To improve your comprehension of volleyball, take the following steps:

- Read units 6-8.
- Consider reading other volleyball coaching books, including those available from ASEP (see the back of this book for more information).
- Contact USA Volleyball at (800) 275-8782 for information.
- Attend volleyball clinics and coaching clinics.
- Talk with other, more experienced, volleyball coaches.
- Observe local college, high school, and youth volleyball games.
- Watch volleyball matches on television.

In addition to having volleyball knowledge, you must implement proper training and safety methods so your players can participate with little risk of injury. Even then, sport injuries will occur. And more often than not, you'll be the first person responding to your players' injuries, so be sure you understand the basic emergency care procedures described in unit 5. Also, read in that unit how to handle more serious sport injury situations.

Outlook

Outlook refers to your perspective and goals—what you are seeking as a coach. The most common coaching objectives are (a) to have fun, (b) to help players develop their physical, mental, and social skills, and (c) to win. Thus your outlook involves the priorities you set, your planning, and your vision for the future.

To work successfully with children in a sport setting, you must have your priorities in order. In just what order do you rank the importance of fun, development, and winning?

Answer the following questions to examine your objectives:

Which situation would make you most proud?

    a. Knowing that each participant enjoyed playing volleyball.

    b. Seeing that all players improved their volleyball skills.

    c. Winning the league championship.

Which statement best reflects your thoughts about sport?

    a. If it isn't fun, don't do it.

    b. Everyone should learn something every day.

    c. Sports aren't fun if you don't win.

How would you like your players to remember you?

   a. As a coach who was fun to play for.

   b. As a coach who provided a good base of fundamental skills.

   c. As a coach who had a winning record.

Which would you most like to hear a parent of a child on your team say?

   a. Billy really had a good time playing volleyball this year.

   b. Susie learned some important lessons playing volleyball this year.

   c. José played on the first-place volleyball team this year.

Which of the following would be the most rewarding moment of your season?

   a. Having your team want to continue playing, even after practice is over.

   b. Seeing one of your players finally master the skill of setting for the hitter.

   c. Winning an important match.

Look over your answers. If you most often selected "a" responses, then having fun is most important to you. A majority of "b" answers suggests that skill development is what attracts you to coaching. And if "c" was your most frequent response, winning tops your list of coaching priorities.

Most coaches say fun and development are more important, but when actually coaching, some coaches emphasize—indeed, over-emphasize—winning. You, too, will face situations that challenge you to keep winning in its proper perspective. During such moments, you'll have to choose between emphasizing your players' development or winning. If your priorities are in order, your players' well-being will take precedence over your team's win-loss record every time.

Take the following actions to better define your outlook:

1. Determine your priorities for the season.
2. Prepare for situations that challenge your priorities.
3. Set goals for yourself and your players that are consistent with those priorities.
4. Plan how you and your players can best attain those goals.
5. Review your goals frequently to be sure that you are staying on track.

It is particularly important for coaches to permit all young athletes to participate. Each youngster—male and female, small and tall, gifted and disabled, skilled and unskilled—should have an opportunity to develop skills and have fun.

Remember that the challenge and joy of sport is experienced through striving to win, not through winning itself. Players who aren't allowed off the bench are denied the opportunity to strive to win. And herein lies the irony: Coaches who allow all of their players to participate and develop skills will—in the end—come out on top.

ASEP has a motto that will help you keep your outlook focused on the best interest of the kids on your team. It summarizes in four words all you need to remember when establishing your coaching priorities:

Athletes First,

Winning Second

This motto recognizes that striving to win is an important, even vital, part of sport. But it emphatically states that no efforts in striving to win should be made at the expense of the athletes' well-being, development, and enjoyment.

Affection

Affection is another vital tool you will want to have in your coaching kit: a genuine concern for the young people you coach. It involves having a love for children, a desire to share that love and your knowledge of volleyball with them, and the patience and understanding that allow each individual playing for you to grow from his or her involvement in sport.

Successful coaches have a real concern for the health and welfare of their players. They care that each child on the team has an enjoyable and successful experience. They recognize that there are similarities between young people's sport experiences and other activities in their lives, and they encourage their players to strive to learn from all their experiences, to become well-rounded individuals. These coaches have a strong desire to work with children and be involved in their growth. And they have the patience to work with those who are slower to learn or less capable of performing. If you have such qualities or are willing to work hard to develop them, then you have the affection necessary to coach young athletes.

There are many ways to demonstrate your affection and patience, including these:

- Make an effort to get to know each player on your team.
- Treat each player as an individual.

- Empathize with players trying to learn new and difficult volleyball skills.
- Treat players as you would like to be treated under similar circumstances.
- Be in control of your emotions.
- Show your enthusiasm for being involved with your team.
- Keep an upbeat and positive tone in all of your communications.

Some children appreciate a pat on the back or shoulder as a sign of your approval or affection. But be aware that not all players feel comfortable with being touched. When this is the case, you need to respect their wishes.

Character

Character is a word that adults use frequently in conversations about sport experiences and young people. If you haven't already, you may one day be asked to explain whether you think sport builds good character. What will you say?

The fact that you have decided to coach young volleyball players probably means that you think participation in sport is important. But whether or not that participation develops character in your players depends as much on you as it does on the sport itself. How can you build character in your players?

Youngsters learn by listening to what adults say. But they learn even more by watching the behavior of certain important individuals. As a coach, you are likely to be a significant figure in the lives of your players. Will you be a good role model?

Having good character means modeling appropriate behaviors for sport and life. That means more than just saying the right things. What you say and what you do must match. There is no place in coaching for the "Do as I say, not as I do" philosophy. Challenge, support, encourage, and reward every child, and your players will be more likely to accept, even celebrate, their differences. Be in control before, during, and after all games and practices. And don't be afraid to admit that you were wrong. No one is perfect!

Many of us have been coached by someone who believes that criticizing players is a good way to build character. In reality, this approach damages children's self-esteem and teaches them that their value as a person is based on how they perform in sport. Unit 3 will help you communicate with your players in a way that builds positive self-esteem and develops your athletes' skills.

Finally, take stock of your own attitudes about ethnic, gender, and other stereotypes. You are an individual coach, and it would be wrong for others to form beliefs about you based on their personal attitudes about coaches in general. Similarly, you need to avoid making comments that support stereotypes of others. Let your words and actions show your players that every individual matters, and you will be teaching them a valuable lesson about respecting and supporting individuals' differences.

Consider the following steps to being a good role model:

- Take stock of your strengths and weaknesses.

- Build on your strengths.

- Set goals for yourself to improve upon those areas you would not like to see mimicked.

- If you slip up, apologize to your team and to yourself. You'll do better next time.

Humor

Humor is an often-overlooked coaching tool. For our use it means having the ability to laugh at yourself and with your players during practices and games. Nothing helps balance the tone of a serious, skill-learning session like a chuckle or two. And a sense of humor puts in perspective the many mistakes your young players will make. So don't get upset over each miscue or respond negatively to erring players. Allow your players and yourself to enjoy the ups, and don't dwell on the downs.

Here are some tips for injecting humor into your practices:

- Make practices fun by including a variety of activities.
- Keep all players involved in drills and scrimmages.
- Consider laughter by your players a sign of enjoyment, not waning discipline.
- Smile!

Where Do You Stand?

To take stock of your "coaching tool kit," rank yourself on the three questions for each of the five coaching tools. Simply circle the number that best describes your current status on each item.

Not at all		Somewhat		Very much so
1	**2**	**3**	**4**	**5**

Comprehension _____

1. Could you explain the rules of volleyball to other parents without studying for a long time?   1 2 3 4 5
2. Do you know how to organize and conduct safe volleyball practices?   1 2 3 4 5
3. Do you know how to provide first aid for most common, minor sport injuries?   1 2 3 4 5

Comprehension Score: _____

Outlook

4. Do you place the interests of all children ahead of winning when you coach? 1 2 3 4 5

5. Do you plan for every meeting and practice? 1 2 3 4 5

6. Do you have a vision of what you want your players to be able to do by the end of the season? 1 2 3 4 5

Outlook Score: _____

Affection

7. Do you enjoy working with children? 1 2 3 4 5

8. Are you patient with youngsters learning new skills? 1 2 3 4 5

9. Are you able to show your players that you care? 1 2 3 4 5

Affection Score: _____

Character

10. Are your words and behaviors consistent with each other? 1 2 3 4 5

11. Are you a good model for your players? 1 2 3 4 5

12. Do you keep negative emotions under control before, during, and after matches and practices? 1 2 3 4 5

Character Score: _____

Humor

13. Do you usually smile at your players? 1 2 3 4 5

14. Are your practices fun? 1 2 3 4 5

15. Are you able to laugh at your mistakes? 1 2 3 4 5

Humor Score: _____

If you scored 9 or less on any of the coaching tools, be sure to reread those sections carefully. And even if you scored 15 on each tool, don't be complacent. Keep learning! Then you'll be well-equipped with the tools you need to coach young athletes.

Unit 3

How Should I Communicate With My Players?

Now you know the tools needed to COACH: Comprehension, Outlook, Affection, Character, and Humor. These are essentials for effective coaching; without them, you'd have a difficult time getting started. But none of those tools will work if you don't know how to use them with your athletes—and this requires skillful communication. This unit examines what communication is and how you can become a more effective communicator and coach.

What's Involved in Communication?

Coaches often mistakenly believe that communication involves only instructing players to do something, but verbal commands are a very small part of the communication process. More than half of what is communicated is nonverbal. So remember when you are coaching: Actions speak louder than words.

Communication in its simplest form involves two people: a sender and a receiver. The sender transmits the message verbally, through facial expression, and possibly through body language. Once the message is sent, the receiver must assimilate it successfully. A receiver who fails to listen will miss parts, if not all, of the message.

How Can I Send More Effective Messages?

Young athletes often have little understanding of the rules and skills of volleyball and probably even less confidence in playing it. So they need accurate, understandable, and supportive messages to help them along. That's why your verbal and nonverbal messages are so important.

Verbal Messages

"Sticks and stones may break my bones, but words will never hurt me" isn't true. Spoken words can have a strong and long-lasting effect. And coaches' words are particularly influential because youngsters place great importance on what coaches say. Perhaps you, like many former youth sport participants, have a difficult time remembering much of anything you were told by your elementary school teachers but can still recall several specific things your coaches at that level said to you. Such is the lasting effect of a coach's comments to a player.

Whether you are correcting misbehavior, teaching a player how to set the ball, or praising a player for good effort, there are a number of things you should consider when sending a message verbally. They include the following:

- *Be positive and honest.*
- *State it clearly and simply.*
- *Say it loud enough, and say it again.*
- *Be consistent.*

Be Positive and Honest

Nothing turns people off like hearing someone nag all the time, and young athletes react similarly to a coach who gripes constantly. Kids particularly need encouragement because they doubt their ability to perform in sport. So look for and tell your players what they did well.

But don't cover up poor or incorrect play with rosy words of praise. Kids know all too well when they've erred, and no cheerfully expressed cliché can undo their mistakes. If you fail to acknowledge players' errors, your athletes will think you are a phony.

State It Clearly and Simply

Positive and honest messages are good, but only if expressed directly in words your players understand. "Beating around the bush" is ineffective and inefficient. And if you do ramble, your players will miss the point of your message and probably lose interest. Here are some tips for saying things clearly.

- Organize your thoughts before speaking to your athletes.
- Explain things thoroughly, but don't bore them with long-winded monologues.
- Use language your players can understand. However, avoid using slang vocabulary in an attempt to be hip.

COMPLIMENT SANDWICH

A good way to handle situations in which you have identified and must correct improper technique is to serve your players a "compliment sandwich":

1. Point out what the athlete did correctly.
2. Let the player know what was incorrect in the performance and instruct him or her how to correct it.
3. Encourage the player by reemphasizing what he or she did well.

Say It Loud Enough, and Say It Again

A crowded gym filled with the sound of bouncing balls can hinder communication, so talk to your team in a voice that all members can hear and interpret. A crisp, vigorous voice commands attention and respect; garbled and weak speech is tuned out. It's appropriate to soften your voice when speaking to a player individually about a personal problem. But most of the time your messages will be for all your players to hear, so make sure they can! An enthusiastic voice also motivates players and tells them you enjoy being their coach. A word of caution, however: Don't dominate the setting with a booming voice that distracts attention from players' performances.

Sometimes what you say, even if stated loud and clear, won't sink in the first time. This may be particularly true with young athletes hearing words they don't understand. To avoid boring repetition and yet still get your message across, say the same thing in a slightly different way. For instance, you might first tell your players "Set the ball to the outside." Soon afterward, remind them "Put the ball in good position for the hitter." The second form of the message may get through to players who missed it the first time around.

Be Consistent

People often say things in ways that imply a different message. For example, a touch of sarcasm added to the words "way to go" sends an entirely different message than the words themselves suggest. It is essential that you avoid sending such mixed messages. Keep the tone of your voice consistent with the words you use. And don't say something one day and contradict it the next; players will get their wires crossed.

Nonverbal Messages

Just as you should be consistent in the tone of voice and words you use, you should also keep your verbal and nonverbal messages consistent. An extreme example of failing to do this would be shaking your head, indicating disapproval, while at the same time telling a player "Nice try." Which is the player to believe, your gesture or your words?

Messages can be sent nonverbally in a number of ways. Facial expressions and body language are just two of the more obvious forms of nonverbal signals that can help you when you coach.

Facial Expressions

The look on a person's face is the quickest clue to what he or she thinks or feels. Your players know this, so they will study your face, looking for any sign that will tell them more than the words you say. Don't try to fool them by putting on a happy or blank "mask." They'll see through it, and you'll lose credibility.

Serious, stone-faced expressions are no help to kids who need cues as to how they are performing. They will just assume you're unhappy or disinterested. Don't be afraid to smile. A smile from a coach can give a great boost to an unsure young athlete. Plus, a smile lets your players know that you are happy coaching them. But don't overdo it, or your players won't be able to tell when you are genuinely pleased by something they've done or when you are just putting on a smiling face.

Body Language

What would your players think you were feeling if you came to practice slouched over, with head down and shoulders slumped? Tired? Bored? Unhappy? What would they think you were feeling if you watched them during a game with your hands on your hips, your jaws clenched, and your face reddened? Upset with them? Disgusted at an official? Mad at a fan? Probably some or all of these things would enter your players' minds. And none of these impressions is the kind you want your players to have of you. That's why you should carry yourself in a pleasant, confident, and vigorous manner. Such a posture not only projects happiness with your coaching role but also provides a good example for your young players, who may model your behavior.

Physical contact can also be a very important use of body language. A handshake, a pat on the head, an arm around the shoulder, or even a big hug are effective ways of showing approval, concern, affection, and joy to your players. Youngsters are especially in need of this type of nonverbal message. Keep within the obvious moral and legal limits, but don't be reluctant to touch your players and send a message that can only truly be expressed in that way.

How Can I Improve My Receiving Skills?

Now, let's examine the other half of the communication process—receiving messages. Too often people are very good senders but very poor receivers of messages. As a coach of young athletes, it is essential that you are able to fulfill both roles effectively.

The requirements for receiving messages are quite simple, but receiving skills are perhaps less satisfying and therefore underdeveloped compared to sending skills. People seem to naturally enjoy hearing themselves talk more than others. But if you are willing to read about the keys to receiving messages and to make a strong effort to use them with your players, you'll be surprised by what you've been missing.

Attention!

First, you must pay attention; you must want to hear what others have to communicate to you. That's not always easy when you're busy coaching and have many things competing for your attention. But in one-to-one or team meetings with players, you must really focus on what they are telling you, both verbally and nonverbally. You'll be amazed at the little signals you pick up. Not only will such focused attention help you catch every word your players say, but you'll also notice your players' moods and physical states, and you'll get an idea of their feelings toward you and other players on the team.

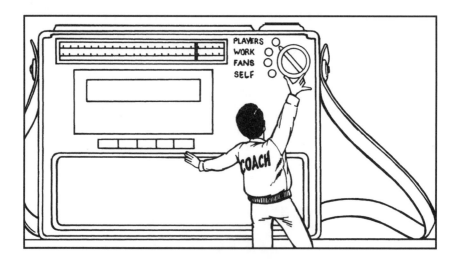

Listen CARE-FULLY

How we receive messages from others, perhaps more than anything else we do, demonstrates how much we care for the sender and what that person has to tell us. If you care little for your players or have little regard for what they have to say, it will show in how you attend and listen to them. Check yourself. Do you find your mind wandering to what you are going to do after practice while one of your players is talking to you? Do you frequently have to ask your players, "What did you say?" If so, you need to work on your receiving mechanics of attending and listening. But perhaps the most critical question you should ask yourself, if you find that you're missing the messages your players send, is this: Do I care?

How Do I Put It All Together?

So far we've discussed separately the sending and receiving of messages. But we all know that senders and receivers switch roles several times during an interaction. One person initiates a communication by sending a message to another person, who then receives the message. The receiver then switches roles and becomes the sender by responding to the person who sent the initial message. These verbal and nonverbal responses are called feedback.

Your players will be looking to you for feedback all the time. They will want to know how you think they are performing, what you think of their ideas, and whether their efforts please you. Obviously, you can respond in many different ways. How you respond will strongly affect your players. So let's take a look at a few general types of feedback and examine their possible effects.

Providing Instructions

With young players, much of your feedback will involve answering questions about how to play volleyball. Your instructive responses to these questions should include both verbal and nonverbal feedback. Here are some suggestions for giving instructional feedback:

- Keep verbal instructions simple and concise.
- Use demonstrations to provide nonverbal instructional feedback (see unit 4).
- "Walk" players through the skill, or use a slow-motion demonstration if they are having trouble learning.

Correcting Errors

When your players perform incorrectly, you need to provide informative feedback to correct the error—and the sooner the better. And when you do correct errors, keep in mind these two principles: Use negative criticism sparingly, and keep calm.

Use Negative Criticism Sparingly

Although you may need to punish players for horseplay or dangerous activities by scolding or removing them from activity temporarily, avoid reprimanding players for performance errors. Admonishing players for honest mistakes makes them afraid to even try. Nothing ruins a youngster's enjoyment of a sport more than a coach who harps on every miscue. So instead, correct your players by using the positive approach. Your players will enjoy playing more, and you'll enjoy coaching more.

Keep Calm

Don't fly off the handle when your players make mistakes. Remember, you're coaching young and inexperienced players, not pros. You'll therefore see more incorrect than correct technique, and you'll probably have more discipline problems than you expect. But throwing a tantrum over each error or misbehavior will only inhibit your players or suggest to them the wrong kind of behavior to model. So let your players know that mistakes aren't the end of the world; stay cool!

Giving Positive Feedback

Praising players when they have performed or behaved well is an effective way of getting them to repeat (or try to repeat) that behavior in the future. And positive feedback for effort is an especially effective way to motivate youngsters to work on difficult skills. So rather than shouting and providing negative feedback to a player who has made a mistake, try offering players a compliment sandwich, described on page 22.

Sometimes just the way you word feedback can make it more positive than negative. For example, instead of saying, "Don't hit the ball that way," you might say, "Hit the ball this way." Then your players will be focusing on what to do instead of what not to do.

Coaches, be positive!

Only a very small percentage of ASEP-trained coaches' behaviors are negative.

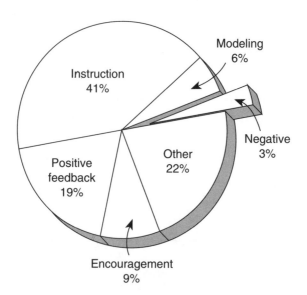

You can give positive feedback verbally and nonverbally. Telling a player, especially in front of teammates, that he or she has performed well is a great way to boost the confidence of a youngster. And a pat on the back or a handshake can be a very tangible way of communicating your recognition of a player's performance.

Who Else Do I Need to Communicate With?

Coaching involves not only sending and receiving messages and providing proper feedback to players, but also interacting with parents, fans, game officials, and opposing coaches. If you don't communicate effectively with these groups of people, your coaching career will be unpleasant and short-lived. So try the following suggestions for communicating with these groups.

Parents

A player's parents need to be assured that their son or daughter is under the direction of a coach who is both knowledgeable about the sport and concerned about the youngster's well-being. You can put their worries to rest by holding a preseason parent orientation meeting in which you describe your background and your approach to coaching.

If parents contact you with a concern during the season, listen to them closely and try to offer positive responses. If you need to communicate with parents, catch them after a practice, give them a phone call, or send a note through the mail. Messages sent to parents through children are too often lost, misinterpreted, or forgotten.

Fans

The stands probably won't be overflowing at your games, but that only means that you'll more easily hear the few fans who criticize your coaching. When you hear something negative said about the job you're doing, don't respond. Keep calm, consider whether the message has any value, and if not, forget it. Acknowledging critical, unwarranted comments from a fan during a game will only encourage others to voice their opinions. So put away your "rabbit ears" and communicate to fans, through your actions, that you are a confident, competent coach.

Prepare your players for fans' criticisms. Tell them it is you, not the spectators, to whom they should listen. If you notice that one of your players is rattled by a fan's comment, reassure the player that your evaluation is more objective and favorable—and the one that counts.

Game Officials

How you communicate with officials will have a great influence on the way your players behave toward them. Therefore, you need to set an example. Greet officials with a handshake, an introduction, and perhaps some casual conversation about the upcoming contest. Indicate your respect for them before, during, and after the game. Don't make nasty remarks, shout, or use disrespectful body gestures. Your players will see you do it, and they'll get the idea that such behavior is appropriate. Plus, if the official hears or sees you, the communication between the two of you will break down.

Opposing Coaches

Make an effort to visit with the coach of the opposing team before the match. Perhaps the two of you can work out a special arrangement for the game, such as matching up players and coordinating substitutions. During the match, don't get into a personal feud with the opposing coach. Remember, it's the kids, not the coaches, who are competing. And by getting along well with the opposing coach, you'll show your players that competition involves cooperation.

✔ *Summary Checklist*

Now, check your coach-communication skills by answering "Yes" or "No" to the following questions.

	Yes	No
1. Are your verbal messages to your players positive and honest?	___	___
2. Do you speak loudly, clearly, and in a language your athletes understand?	___	___
3. Do you remember to repeat instructions to your players, in case they didn't hear you the first time?	___	___
4. Are the tone of your voice and your nonverbal messages consistent with the words you use?	___	___
5. Do your facial expressions and body language express interest in and happiness with your coaching role?	___	___
6. Are you attentive to your players and able to pick up even their small verbal and nonverbal cues?	___	___
7. Do you really care about what your athletes say to you?	___	___
8. Do you instruct rather than criticize when your players make errors?	___	___
9. Are you usually positive when responding to things your athletes say and do?	___	___
10. Do you try to communicate in a cooperative and respectful manner with players' parents, fans, game officials, and opposing coaches?	___	___

If you answered "No" to any of the above questions, you may want to refer back to the section of the chapter where the topic was discussed. Now is the time to address communication problems, not when you're coaching young athletes.

Unit 4

How Do I Get My Team Ready to Play?

To coach volleyball, you must understand the basic rules, skills, and strategies of the sport. The second part of this book provides the basic information you'll need to comprehend the sport.

But all the volleyball knowledge in the world will do you little good unless you present it effectively to your players. That's why this unit is so important. Here you will learn the steps to take when teaching volleyball skills, as well as practical guidelines for planning your season and individual practices.

How Do I Teach Sport Skills?

Many people believe that the only qualification needed to coach is to have played the sport. It's helpful to have played, but there is much more to coaching successfully. Even if you haven't played or watched volleyball, you can still learn to coach successfully with this IDEA:

I—Introduce the skill.

D—Demonstrate the skill.

E—Explain the skill.

A—Attend to players practicing the skill.

Introduce the Skill

Players, especially young and inexperienced ones, need to know what skill they are learning and why they are learning it. You should therefore take these three steps every time you introduce a skill to your players:

1. Get your players' attention.

2. Name the skill.

3. Explain the importance of the skill.

Get Your Players' Attention

Because youngsters are easily distracted, use some method to get their attention. Some coaches use interesting news items or stories. Others use jokes. And others simply project enthusiasm that gets their players to listen. Whatever method you use, speak slightly above the normal volume and look your players in the eyes when you speak.

Also, position players so they can see and hear you. Arrange the players in two or three evenly spaced rows, facing you and not some source of distraction. Then ask if all can see and hear you before you begin.

Name the Skill

Although you might mention other common names for the skill, decide which one you'll use and stick with it. This will help avoid confusion and enhance communication among your players. For example, choose either "bump" or "dig" as the term for the forearm passing skill, and use it consistently.

Explain the Importance of the Skill

Although the importance of a skill may be apparent to you, your players may be less able to see how the skill will help them become better volleyball players. Offer them a reason for learning the skill and describe how the skill relates to more advanced skills.

> *"The most difficult aspect of coaching is this: Coaches must learn to let athletes learn. Sport skills should be taught so they have meaning to the child, not just meaning to the coach."*
>
> Rainer Martens, ASEP Founder

Demonstrate the Skill

The demonstration step is the most important part of teaching sport skills to young players who may have never done anything closely resembling the skill. They need a picture, not just words. They need to see how the skill is performed.

If you are unable to perform the skill correctly, have an assistant coach, one of your players, or someone skilled in volleyball perform the demonstration. These tips will help make your demonstrations more effective:

- Use correct form.
- Demonstrate the skill several times.
- Slow down the action, if possible, during one or two performances so players can see every movement involved in the skill.
- Perform the skill at different angles so your players can get a full perspective of it.
- Demonstrate the skill from both the right and left sides and each end of the court.

Explain the Skill

Players learn more effectively when they're given a brief explanation of the skill along with the demonstration. Use simple terms and, if possible, relate the skill to previously learned skills. Ask your players whether they understand your description. A good technique is to ask the team to repeat your explanation. Ask questions like "What are you going to do first?" "Then what?" Watch for looks of confusion or uncertainty and repeat your explanation and demonstration of

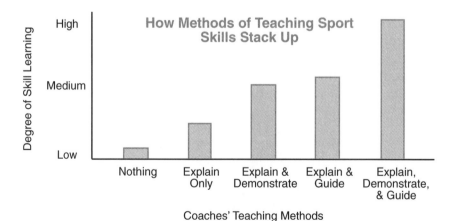

Coaches' Teaching Methods

those points. If possible, use different words so that your players get a chance to try to understand from a different perspective.

Complex skills often are better understood when they are explained in more manageable parts. For instance, if you want to teach your players how to serve, you might take the following steps:

1. Show them a correct performance of the entire skill and explain its function in volleyball.
2. Break down the skill and point out its component parts to your players.
3. Have players perform each of the component skills you have already taught them, such as preparation, toss, precontact movement, and contact.
4. After players have demonstrated their ability to perform the separate parts of the skill in sequence, reexplain the entire skill.
5. Have players practice the skill.

One caution: Young players have short attention spans, and a long demonstration or explanation of the skill will bore them. So spend no more than a few minutes combined on the introduction, demonstration, and explanation phases. Then get the players active in attempts to perform the skill by playing some type of game. The total IDEA should be completed in 10 minutes or less, followed by individual and group practice activities.

Attend to Players Practicing the Skill

If the skill you selected was within your players' capabilities and you have done an effective job of introducing, demonstrating, and explaining it, your players should be ready to attempt the skill. Some players may need to be physically guided through the movements during their first few attempts. Walking unsure athletes through the skill will help them gain confidence to perform it on their own.

Your teaching duties don't end when all your athletes have demonstrated that they understand how to perform the skill. In fact, a significant part of your teaching will involve observing closely the hit-and-miss trial performances of your players.

As you observe players' efforts in drills and activities, offer positive, corrective feedback in the form of the "compliment sandwich"

described in unit 3. If a player performs the skill properly, acknowledge it and offer praise. Keep in mind that your feedback will have a great influence on your players' motivation to practice and improve their performance.

Remember, too, that young players need individual instruction. So set aside a time before, during, or after practice to give individual help.

What Planning Do I Need to Do?

Beginning coaches often make the mistake of showing up for the first practice with no particular plan in mind. These coaches find that their practices are unorganized, their players are frustrated and inattentive, and the amount and quality of their skill instruction is limited. Planning is essential to successful teaching and coaching. And it doesn't begin on the way to practice!

Preseason Planning

Effective coaches begin planning well before the start of the season. Among the preseason measures that will make the season more enjoyable, successful, and safe for you and your players are the following:

- Familiarize yourself with the sport organization you are involved in, especially its philosophy and goals regarding youth sport.

- Examine the availability of facilities, equipment, instructional aids, and other materials needed for practices and matches.
- Find out what fund-raising you and your players will be expected to do, and decide on the best way to meet your goals.
- Make arrangements for any team travel that will be required during the season. Consider clearance forms, supervision, transportation, equipment, contacting parents, and safety.
- Check to see whether you have adequate liability insurance to cover you when one of your players is hurt (see unit 5). If you don't, get some.
- Establish your coaching priorities regarding having fun, developing players' skills, and winning.
- Select and meet with your assistant coaches to discuss the philosophy, goals, team rules, and plans for the season.
- Register players for the team. Have them complete a player information form and obtain medical clearance forms, if required.
- Institute an injury-prevention program for your players.
- Hold an orientation meeting to inform parents of your background, philosophy, goals, and instructional approach. Also, give a brief overview of volleyball rules, terms, and strategies to familiarize parents or guardians with the sport.

You may be surprised at the number of things you should do even before the first practice. But if you address them during the preseason, the season will be much more enjoyable and productive for you and your players.

In-Season Planning

Your choice of activities during the season should be based on whether they will help your players develop physical and mental skills, knowledge of rules and game tactics, sportsmanship, and love for the sport. All of these goals are important, but we'll focus on the skills and tactics of volleyball to give you an idea of how to itemize your objectives.

Goal Setting

What you plan to do during the season must be reasonable for the maturity and skill levels of your players. In terms of volleyball skills and tactics, you should teach young players the basics and move on to more complex activities only after the players have mastered these easier techniques and strategies.

To begin the season, your instructional goals might include the following:

- Players will be able to use proper footwork when moving to the ball.
- Players will be able to assume and recover to ready position.
- Players will be able to serve the ball to specific areas of the court using the underhand and overhand serves.

- Players will be able to forearm pass correctly to the setter's position.
- Players will be able to correctly set to the hitter's position.
- Players will be able to attack the ball to specific areas of the court.
- Players will be able to execute the proper footwork and hand position for blocking an attack.
- Players will be able to use proper technique for digging an attacked ball.
- Players will demonstrate knowledge of basic offensive and defensive strategies.
- Players will demonstrate knowledge of volleyball playing rules.
- Players will be able to communicate effectively on the court with teammates.

Organizing

After you've defined the skills and tactics you want your players to learn during the season, you can plan how to teach them to your players in practices. But be flexible! If your players are having difficulty learning a skill or tactic, take some extra time until they get the hang of it—even if that means moving back your schedule. After all, if your players are unable to perform the fundamental skills, they'll never execute the more complex skills you have scheduled for them, and they won't have much fun trying.

Still, it helps to have a plan for progressing players through skills during the season. The 4-week sample season plan in appendix B shows how to schedule your skill instruction in an organized and progressive manner. If this is your first coaching experience, you may wish to follow the plan as it stands. If you have some previous experience, you may want to modify the schedule to better fit the needs of your team.

The way you organize your season may also help your players to develop socially and psychologically. By giving your players responsibility for certain aspects of practices—leading warm-up and stretching activities are common examples—you help them develop self-esteem and take responsibility for themselves and the team. As you plan your season, consider ways to provide your players with experiences that lead them to steadily improve these skills.

What Makes Up a Good Practice?

A good instructional plan makes practice preparation much easier. Have players work on more important and less difficult goals in early-season practice sessions. And see to it that players master basic skills before moving on to more advanced ones.

It is helpful to establish one goal for each practice, but try to include a variety of activities related to that goal. For example, although your primary objective might be to improve players' setting skills, you should have them perform several different drills designed to enhance that single skill. To add more variety to your practices, vary the order of the activities.

In general, we recommend that in each of your practices you do the following:

- *Warm up.*
- *Practice previously taught skills.*
- *Teach and practice new skills.*
- *Practice under competitive conditions.*
- *Cool down.*
- *Evaluate.*

Warm Up

As you're checking the roster and announcing the performance goals for the practice, your players should be preparing their bodies for vigorous activity. A 5- to 10-minute period of easy-paced activities, stretching, and calisthenics should be sufficient for youngsters to limber their muscles and reduce the risk of injury.

Practice Previously Taught Skills

Devote part of each practice to having players work on the fundamental skills they already know. But remember, kids like variety. Thus, you should organize and modify drills so that everyone is involved and stays interested. Praise and encourage players when you notice improvement, and offer individual assistance to those who need help.

Teach and Practice New Skills

Gradually build on your players' existing skills by giving players something new to practice each session. The proper method for teaching sport skills is described on pages 36–40. Refer to those pages if you have any questions about teaching new skills or if you want to evaluate your teaching approach periodically during the season.

Practice Under Competitive Conditions

Competition among teammates during practices prepares players for actual games and informs young athletes about their abilities relative to their peers. Youngsters also seem to have more fun in competitive activities.

You can create game-like conditions by using competitive drills, modified games, and scrimmages (see units 7 and 8). However, consider the following guidelines before introducing competition into your practices:

- All players should have an equal opportunity to participate.
- Match players by ability and physical maturity.
- Make sure that players can execute fundamental skills before they compete in groups.

- Emphasize performing well, not winning, in every competition.

- Give players room to make mistakes by avoiding constant evaluation of their performances.

Cool Down

Each practice should wind down with a 5- to 10-minute period of light exercise, including jogging, performance of simple skills, and some stretching. The cool-down allows athletes' bodies to return to the resting state and avoid stiffness, and it affords you an opportunity to review the practice.

Evaluate

At the end of practice spend a few minutes with your players reviewing how well the session accomplished the goals you had set. Even if your evaluation is negative, show optimism for future practices and send players off on an upbeat note.

How Do I Put a Practice Together?

Simply knowing the six practice components is not enough. You must also be able to arrange those components into a logical progression and fit them into a time schedule. Now, using your instructional goals as a guide for selecting what skills to have your players work on, try to plan several volleyball practices you might conduct. The following example should help you get started.

Sample Practice Plan

Performance Objective. Players will be able to pass effectively and accurately with both the forearm and overhead passes.

Component	Time	Activity or drill
Warm up	10 min	Light running Calisthenics/stretching
Practice previously taught skills	15 min	Practice tossing skills Toss and pass to self
Teach	15 min	Forearm and overhead passes to a partner
Practice	20 min	Triangle Passing Drill Free-Ball Overhead Passing Drill
Scrimmage	15 min	3-on-3 modified scrimmage (points awarded for each pass to the setter)
Cool down and evaluate	10 min	Serving Stretching

✔ *Summary Checklist*

During your volleyball season, check your planning and teaching skills periodically. As you gain more coaching experience, you should be able to answer "Yes" to each of the following.

When you plan, do you remember to plan for

_____ preseason events such as player registration, fund-raising, travel, liability protection, use of facilities, and parent orientation?

_____ season goals such as the development of players' physical skills, mental skills, sportsmanship, and enjoyment?

_____ practice components such as warm-up, practicing previously taught skills, teaching and practicing new skills, practicing under game-like conditions, cool-down, and evaluation?

When you teach sport skills to your players, do you

_____ arrange the players so all can see and hear?

_____ introduce the skill clearly and explain its importance?

_____ demonstrate the skill properly several times?

_____ explain the skill simply and accurately?

_____ attend closely to players practicing the skill?

_____ offer corrective, positive feedback or praise after observing players' attempts at the skill?

Unit 5

What About Safety?

One of your players reacts quickly to the ball, diving to dig a spike hit toward the sideline. Incredibly, your player digs the ball to a teammate and saves the point. But just as you turn to praise the gutsy play, you see that the player is still down on the court. She is clutching her elbow and seems to be in pain. What do you do?

No coach wants to see players get hurt. But injury remains a reality of sport participation; consequently, you must be prepared to provide first aid when injuries occur and to protect yourself against unjustified lawsuits. Fortunately, there are many preventive measures coaches can institute to reduce the risk. This unit will describe how you can

- create the safest possible environment for your players,
- provide emergency first aid to players when they get hurt, and
- protect yourself from injury liability.

How Do I Keep My Players From Getting Hurt?

Injuries may occur because of poor preventive measures. Part of your planning, described in unit 4, should include steps that give your players the best possible chance for injury-free participation. These steps include the following:

- *Preseason physical examination*
- *Nutrition*
- *Physical conditioning*
- *Apparel and facilities inspection*
- *Matching athletes by physical maturity and warning of inherent risks*
- *Proper supervision and record keeping*
- *Providing water breaks*
- *Warm-up and cool-down*

Preseason Physical Examination

In the absence of severe injury or ongoing illness, your players should have a physical examination every two years. If a player has a known complication, a physician's consent should be obtained before participation is allowed. You should also have players' parents or guardians sign a participation agreement form and a release form to allow their children to be treated in case of an emergency.

INFORMED CONSENT FORM

I hereby give my permission for _____ to participate

in _____ during the athletic season beginning in 199____.
Further, I authorize the school to provide emergency treatment of an injury to or illness of my child if qualified medical personnel consider treatment necessary *and* perform the treatment. This authorization is granted only if I cannot be reached and a reasonable effort has been made to do so.

Date _____   Parent or guardian _____

Address _____ Phone ( ) _____

Family physician _____ Phone ( ) _____

Pre-existing medical conditions (e.g., allergies or chronic illnesses) _____

_____

Other(s) to also contact in case of emergency _____

Relationship to child _____ Phone ( ) _____

My child and I are aware that participating in _____
is a potentially hazardous activity. I assume all risks associated with participation in this sport, including but not limited to falls, contact with other participants, the effects of the weather, traffic, and other reasonable risk conditions associated with the sport. All such risks to my child are known and understood by me.

I understand this informed consent form and agree to its conditions on behalf of my child.

Child's signature _____ Date _____

Parent's signature _____ Date _____

Nutrition

Increasingly, disordered eating and unhealthy dietary habits are affecting youth volleyball players. Let players and parents know the importance of healthy eating and the dangers that can arise from efforts to lose weight too quickly. Young volleyball players need to supply their bodies with the extra energy they need to keep up with the demands of practices and games. Ask your director about information that you can pass on to your players and their parents, and include a discussion of basic, commonsense nutrition in your parent orientation meeting.

Physical Conditioning

Muscles, tendons, and ligaments unaccustomed to vigorous and long-lasting physical activity are prone to injury. Therefore, prepare your athletes to withstand the exertion of playing volleyball. An effective conditioning program for volleyball would involve running, lateral movement, and jumping activities.

Make conditioning drills and activities fun. Include a skill component, such as serving or passing, to prevent players from becoming bored or looking upon the activity as work.

Keep in mind, too, that players on your team may respond differently to conditioning activities. Wide-ranging levels of fitness or natural ability might mean that an activity that challenges one child is beyond another's ability to complete safely. The environment is another factor that may affect players' responses to activity. The same workout that was effective on a cool morning might be hazardous to players on a hot, humid afternoon. Similarly, an activity children excel in at sea level might present a risk at higher altitudes. An ideal conditioning program prepares players for the season's demands without neglecting physical and environmental factors that affect their safety.

Apparel and Facilities Inspection

Another way to prevent injuries is to check the quality and fit of the clothes that your players wear. Slick-soled, poor fitting, or unlaced volleyball shoes; unstrapped eyeglasses; and jewelry are dangerous on the volleyball court. Also, encourage players to carry their volleyball shoes to practice and game sites so that the soles of their shoes are free of mud and moisture.

Remember, also, to examine regularly the court on which your players practice and play. Wipe up wet spots, remove hazards, report conditions you cannot remedy, and request maintenance as necessary. If unsafe conditions exist, either make adaptations to avoid risk to your players' safety or stop the practice or match until safe conditions have been restored.

Matching Athletes by Physical Maturity and Warning of Inherent Risks

Children of the same age may differ in height and weight by up to 6 inches and 50 pounds. That's why in volleyball, where size provides such an advantage, it's essential to match players against opponents of similar physical maturity and size. Such an approach gives smaller, less mature children a better chance to succeed and avoid injury, and provides larger children with more of a challenge.

Matching helps protect you from certain liability concerns. But you also must warn players of the inherent risks involved in playing volleyball, because "failure to warn" is one of the most successful arguments in lawsuits against coaches. So, thoroughly explain the inherent risks of volleyball and make sure each player knows, understands, and appreciates those risks.

The preseason parent orientation meeting is a good opportunity to explain the risks of the sport to parents and players. It is also a good occasion on which to have both the players and their parents sign waivers releasing you from liability should an injury occur. (See a sample informed consent form on page 51). Such waivers do not relieve you of responsibility for your players' well-being, but they are recommended by lawyers.

Proper Supervision and Record Keeping

With youngsters, your mere presence in the area of play is not enough; you must actively plan and direct team activities and closely observe and evaluate players' participation. You're the watchdog responsible for the players' well-being. So if you notice a player limping or grimacing, give him or her a rest and examine the extent of the injury.

As a coach, you're also required to enforce the rules of the sport, prohibit dangerous horseplay, and hold practices only under safe conditions. These specific supervisory activities will make the play environment safer for your players and will help protect you from liability if a mishap does occur.

For further protection, keep records of your season plans, practice plans, and players' injuries. Season and practice plans come in handy when you need evidence that players have been taught certain skills, and accurate, detailed accident report forms offer protection against unfounded lawsuits. Ask for these forms from the organization to which you belong. And hold onto these records for several years so that an "old volleyball injury" of a former player doesn't come back to haunt you.

Providing Water Breaks

Encourage players to drink plenty of water before, during, and after practices and games. Because water makes up 45% to 65% of a youngster's body weight and water weighs about a pound per pint, the loss of even a little bit of water can have severe consequences for the body's systems. And it doesn't have to be hot and humid for players to become dehydrated. Nor do players have to feel thirsty; in fact, by the time they are aware of their thirst, they are long overdue for a drink.

Warm-Up and Cool-Down

Although young bodies are generally very limber, they, too, can get tight from inactivity. Therefore, a warm-up period of about 10 minutes before each practice is strongly recommended. Warm-up should address each muscle group and get the heart rate elevated in preparation for strenuous activity. Easy running followed by stretching activities is a common sequence.

As practice is winding down, slow players' heart rates with easy jogging or walking. Then arrange for a 5- to 10-minute period of easy stretching at the end of practice to help players avoid stiff muscles and make them less tight before the next practice.

What if One of My Players Gets Hurt?

No matter how good and thorough your prevention program, injuries will occur. When injury does strike, chances are you will be the one in charge. The severity and nature of the injury will determine how actively involved you'll be in treating the injury. But regardless of how seriously a player is hurt, it is your responsibility to know what steps to take. So let's look at how you can provide basic emergency care to your injured athletes.

Minor Injuries

Although no injury seems minor to the person experiencing it, most injuries are neither life-threatening nor severe enough to restrict participation. When such injuries occur, you can take an active role in their initial treatment.

ASEP Fact

You shouldn't let a fear of acquired immune deficiency syndrome (AIDS) stop you from helping a player. On the court you are only at risk if you allow contaminated blood to come in contact with an open wound, so the blood barrier that you wear will protect you from AIDS should one of your players carry this disease. Check with your director or ASEP for more information about protecting yourself and your participants from AIDS.

Scrapes and Cuts

When one of your players has an open wound, the first thing you should do is to put on a pair of disposable surgical gloves or some other effective blood barrier. Then follow these four steps:

1. <u>Stop the bleeding</u> by applying direct pressure with a clean dressing to the wound and elevating it. The player may be able to apply this pressure while you put on your gloves. Do not remove the dressing if it becomes soaked with blood. Instead, place an additional dressing on top of the one already in place. If bleeding continues, elevate the injured area above the heart and maintain pressure.

2. <u>Cleanse the wound</u> thoroughly once the bleeding is controlled. A good rinsing with a forceful stream of water, and perhaps light scrubbing with soap, will help prevent infection.

3. <u>Protect the wound</u> with sterile gauze or a bandage. If the player continues to participate, apply protective padding over the injured area.

4. <u>Remove and dispose</u> of gloves carefully to prevent you or anyone else from coming into contact with blood.

For bloody noses not associated with serious facial injury, have the athlete sit and lean slightly forward. Then pinch the player's nostrils shut. If the bleeding continues after several minutes, or if the athlete has a history of nosebleeds, seek medical assistance.

Strains and Sprains

The physical demands of volleyball practices and games often result in injury to the muscles or tendons (strains), or to the ligaments (sprains). When your players suffer minor strains or sprains, immediately apply the PRICE method of injury care.

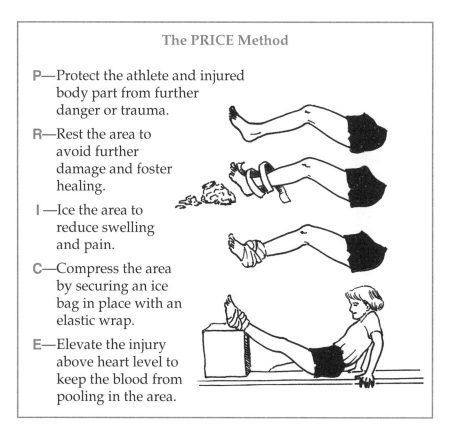

The PRICE Method

P—Protect the athlete and injured body part from further danger or trauma.

R—Rest the area to avoid further damage and foster healing.

I—Ice the area to reduce swelling and pain.

C—Compress the area by securing an ice bag in place with an elastic wrap.

E—Elevate the injury above heart level to keep the blood from pooling in the area.

Bumps and Bruises

Inevitably, volleyball players make contact with the hard court surface. If the force of a body part at impact is great enough, a bump or bruise will result. Many players continue playing with such sore spots, but if the bump or bruise is large and painful, you should act appropriately. Enact the PRICE method for injury care and monitor the injury. If swelling, discoloration, and pain have lessened, the player may resume participation with protective padding; if not, the player should be examined by a physician.

Serious Injuries

Head, neck, and back injuries; fractures; and injuries that cause a player to lose consciousness are among a class of injuries that you cannot and should not try to treat yourself. But you should plan for what you'd do if such an injury occurs. And your plan should include the following guidelines for action:

- Obtain the phone number and ensure the availability of nearby emergency care units. Include this information as part of a written emergency plan before the season, and have it with you at every practice and match.

- Assign an assistant coach or another adult the responsibility of knowing the location of the nearest phone and contacting emergency medical help upon your request.

- Ensure that emergency medical information, treatment, and transportation consent forms are available during every practice and match.

- Do not move the injured athlete.

- Calm the injured athlete and keep others away from him or her as much as possible.

- Evaluate whether the athlete's breathing is stopped or irregular, and if necessary, clear the airway with your fingers.

- Administer artificial respiration if breathing is stopped. Administer cardiopulmonary resuscitation (CPR), or have a trained individual administer CPR, if the athlete's circulation has stopped.

- Remain with the athlete until medical personnel arrive.

How Do I Protect Myself?

When one of your players is injured, naturally your first concern is his or her well-being. Your feelings for children, after all, are what made you decide to coach. Unfortunately, there is something else that you must consider: Can you be held liable for the injury?

From a legal standpoint, a coach has nine duties to fulfill. We've discussed all but planning (see unit 4) in this unit:

1. Provide a safe environment.

2. Properly plan the activity.

3. Provide adequate and proper equipment.

4. Match or equate athletes.

5. Warn of inherent risks in the sport.

6. Supervise the activity closely.

7. Evaluate athletes for injury or incapacitation.

8. Know emergency procedures and first aid.

9. Keep adequate records.

In addition to fulfilling these nine legal duties, you should check your insurance coverage to make sure your policy will protect you from liability.

Summary Self-Test

Now that you've read how to make your coaching experience safe for your players and yourself, test your knowledge of the material by answering these questions:

1. What are eight injury-prevention measures you can institute to try to keep your players from getting hurt?
2. What is the four-step emergency care process for cuts?
3. What method of treatment is best for minor sprains and strains?
4. What steps can you take to manage serious injuries?
5. What are the nine legal duties of a coach?

Unit 6

What Is Volleyball All About?

Volleyball is an exciting game, mixing finesse with power. At all levels of competition, the game requires basic skills and teamwork. In most cases, you'll be the first coach to teach your players the basic skills and strategies of the sport. In the remaining three units of *Coaching Youth Volleyball*, you'll learn the basic rules, court layout, skills, and drills—as well as some helpful hints—for teaching your young athletes how to play this fast and exciting game.

You'll see that the rules and procedures of youth volleyball differ from those for the standard six-on-six game. Many of the same fundamentals apply, but youth volleyball is designed specifically for kids to give them a successful introduction to the sport and to provide enjoyment. With a little training and a lot of enthusiasm, you can help them enjoy volleyball this season and throughout their lives.

Coaching Youth Volleyball

Youth volleyball has its origins in mini-volleyball, where kids play for fun and modify the rules to fit their needs. Your players will be looking for that same kind of fun in the more structured setting of youth volleyball, so keep that in mind when you plan for the season.

ASEP Fact

A recent survey of 10- to 14-year-old athletes showed that more than 90 percent of them would like their sport just as much if no score were kept at all!

Youth volleyball is a unique and effective way to teach volleyball to both young and adult beginners. It has all the components of six-on-six volleyball, but the game is modified to better fit the skills of beginning players. Youth volleyball uses

- a smaller court,
- a lower net,
- lighter, larger balls, and
- two, three, or four players on a side.

A smaller court helps you overcome a gym's space limitations. A gym with two regular-sized volleyball courts has room for four youth courts, and as many as eight teams could use this space very effectively. The court's dimensions can be modified to make the game suitable for all ages and skill levels.

By lowering the net, even small children can learn to spike and block. Kids—just like adults—love being able to perform these two exciting skills. The use of a larger, lighter ball helps beginning players develop specific skills more readily. The ball stays in the air longer, allowing time for players to react and maintain rallies.

In youth volleyball, teams consist of two, three, or four players playing at a time, with substitutes rotating in from the sidelines. With smaller teams and continuous substitutions all players get more playing time and more contacts with the ball. Therefore, youth volleyball enables kids to learn the game more quickly than they would in the version for six-player teams.

Coaching youth sport is a great way to share your knowledge and enthusiasm for volleyball with kids. Don't be discouraged at the start—balls will be bouncing everywhere, but that's part of learning! In youth volleyball, you break down the game into its basic components so beginners can learn while having fun. The modified rules and court help players develop quickly, and the modifications enhance their motivation to improve skills. To prepare you for the challenge of teaching kids how to play volleyball, read the rest of this guide and get ready to pass, set, and spike!

Approaches to Volleyball

Many approaches to volleyball exist, the variations primarily being in the playing surface and numbers of players per side. The most common forms of playing surfaces are hard court (indoor and outdoor), grass, and beach. These playing surfaces make a game possible under virtually any condition, in any climate, and at any time of day. We will explain the differences between each surface, giving an overview also of the benefits and disadvantages of each.

Hard-Court Volleyball

Hard-court volleyball, whether in- or outdoors, provides numerous opportunities to play. Whether in local YMCAs or churches, most recreation facilities are equipped for hard surface volleyball. Hard-court surfaces allow for the development of all the skills in volleyball, with the possible exception of such defensive skills as diving, collapsing, or extension rolls to the ground.

Grass Volleyball

Grass volleyball is enjoying widespread popularity across the country. A level, grass surface—coupled with proper outdoor equipment—can provide a great site to develop skills of volleyball and ensure lifelong enjoyment of the game. As in indoor and beach volleyball, grass volleyball allows optimal development of all skills. Proponents of grass volleyball feel the learning of defensive movements like diving can best be learned outside on the grass where there is no cause to fear landing on hard surfaces.

Beach Volleyball

Beach volleyball is gaining tremendous popularity. A great vehicle for the development of all skills, beach volleyball will likely enjoy continued popularity among all people, whether beginners or beach professionals. Like grass volleyball, it offers a primary benefit over indoor play: the development of defensive skills. While some beginning players hesitate to throw themselves to the floor on a hard surface (in- or outdoors), players feel more secure in learning these skills on a sandy surface and often welcome opportunities to try them out. Encourage and reward that attitude in your athletes.

Comparing Surfaces

Whether learning the individual skills of volleyball on the beach, grass, or indoors, repetition is the key to success. Getting the opportunity to respond in playing situations will allow your novices to develop all skills, regardless of the surface. And there are several similarities among beach, hard-court, and grass volleyball. The techniques for performing skills, such as passing and hitting, remain the same, whatever the court. Athletes have to get used to the differences they feel on the various playing surfaces, yet develop the skills of the game. So players who develop the skills on one surface still can enjoy continued success playing on other, less familiar surfaces.

Learning all skills efficiently, then, is an advantage common to all the playing surfaces. And in volleyball, regardless of where you play, the opportunity is available to learn all basic skills of the game. Outdoor surfaces bring young volleyball players the added difficulty of weather conditions, an aspect not present in the indoor game. Being unfamiliar with wind and sun conditions is an added difficulty to beginning players just learning basic skills, such as passing and hitting. A player who has learned skills primarily in an indoor setting may feel less effective outdoors, when faced with additional weather elements.

You will find that hard indoor surfaces are most suitable for six-player games, whereas two-, three-, and four-player team games are the more popular versions on outdoor surfaces. Because of the different movement requirements on softer court surfaces, like sand and grass, court sizes should be modified for beginners so they can learn skills and enjoy the game more.

What Are the Rules?

Modified rules help players at all levels enjoy games appropriate to their developmental needs. As you see in table 6.1, the court is smaller and the net is lower in youth volleyball. Depending on your league's rules, your team may be playing with two to six players.

Court Dimensions

The standard six-on-six game is played by two teams on a court that measures 59 feet by 29.5 feet, so teams play on a court measuring about 30 feet by 30 feet. In youth volleyball, typically, two three-player teams play on a court measuring 15 feet by 15 feet. You can use different court sizes, depending on your needs. By modifying the regulation dimensions (see figure 6.1, a-c), you can easily set up a court for young players. In general, beginners will have more success on a short, wide court (see figure 6.1, a and b). Older, bigger, and taller players will enjoy playing on a longer, wider court (see figure 6.1c).

Classification	Youth (co-ed)			Junior	Adult
Age/year	6-8	8-10	10-12	12-18	18 and older
Court dimensions	12' × 12'	15' × 15'	20' × 20'	30' × 30'	30' × 30'
Net height	6'1"	6'1"	7'4-1/8"	7'4-1/8" for women and boys aged 12-14 7'11-5/8" for men	
Number of players	2	3	4	6	

Table 6.1 Volleyball Rules

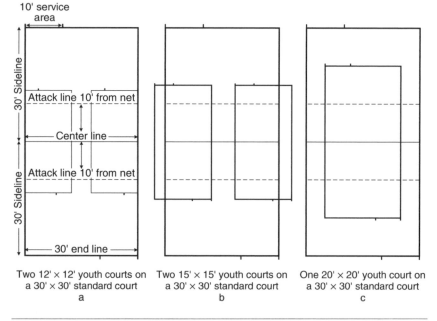

Two 12' × 12' youth courts on a 30' × 30' standard court
a

Two 15' × 15' youth courts on a 30' × 30' standard court
b

One 20' × 20' youth court on a 30' × 30' standard court
c

■ **Figure 6.1** Three modifications of the standard court for youth volleyball.

Here are some recommended court sizes.

- For four versus four— 20 feet by 20 feet
- For three versus three—15 feet by 15 feet
- For two versus two—12 feet by 12 feet

Regardless of whether your team plays on grass, beach, or hard-court surfaces, these court sizes are appropriate. The players' enjoyment of the game on all these surfaces will increase because they can keep balls in play more. With a smaller court area to cover, they don't have far to go to make the next contact.

Court Markings

All lines marking the playing area on hard courts are two inches wide. Sporting goods stores and volleyball supply companies carry plastic tape especially made for marking volleyball courts on gym floors. Court markings on grass and beach surfaces usually are made of rope, which marks the perimeter of the court. The ropes are secured with stakes or other similar items that delineate the court while also maintaining the safety of the environment for the participants. Ensure that the stakes you use can be placed in the ground without potentially tripping an athlete, which could lead to serious injury; follow the manufacturer's instructions! Balls landing on the lines are in bounds in volleyball, so when marking court dimensions, measure from the outside of the lines.

Usually, for playing two versus two, three versus three, or four versus four you do not use the attack line because all the players, whether in the front- or backcourt, can attack the ball (see figure 6.1a). If your team is playing six versus six, however, it would use the attack line. Place the marking about 10 feet from the net on each side of the court. It is not common to use the attack line on grass or beach surfaces.

Net Height

A net divides the court in half. You can vary its height to be appropriate to the skills you are teaching. A higher net makes players set and hit the ball higher and more softly. For beginners, this creates a slower-paced game, with more volleys and contacts for each player.

Using a higher net in practices will give players more time to move and react to the ball. For youth games, the net is set between 6 feet 1 inch and 7 feet 4-1/8 inches, depending on the participants' ages and the height of the tallest players. Regardless of the court surface, the average net height in youth volleyball is set at 6 feet 6 inches. See table 6.1 for net heights.

Balls

The most commonly used volleyball for all levels of volleyball, from youth to juniors to adults, is the size 5 (see table 6.2). For younger ages and even adult beginners, USA Volleyball recommends a special light-weight, low-impact ball. For youth on small courts you might also consider using an oversized ball. To teach skills and vary the learning environment, you can also use balls with "elephant" or "alligator" skin covering, and even punch balloons, beach balls, or rubber-bladder balls with durable, thin-foam coatings. All these balls are widely available from volleyball outlets. Check with your league administrators to see what kind of ball they recommend you use.

Table 6.2 Types of Volleyballs				
Ball Type	**Size**	**Weight**	**Special Features**	**Age Group**
Standard	#5	9-10 oz.	Leather/ synthetic	12 and older
Standard light	#5	8.75 oz.	Synthetic leather	10 and older
Oversized	#6	9 oz.	Synthetic leather	8-12 years
Foam over rubber	#5 and #6	Varies	Foam-covered soft rubber ball	up to 10 years
Foam	#4 and #5	Varies	Dense foam, rough surface	6-8 years
Foam	#4 and #5	Varies	"Elephant skin" surface	6-8 years
Beach ball	Varies	Varies	Plastic	6-8 years

And to make the best possible choice in balls consider the environment you will be playing in.

Ideally, each player should have his or her own volleyball to make it easy to practice at home. This gives players a chance to become more familiar with the weight and feel of the ball. Most sporting goods stores carry volleyballs in a variety of colors, weights, and sizes for indoor or outdoor use.

Player Equipment

Individual player equipment is inexpensive and, like volleyballs, fairly easy to obtain. Here's a list of what your players will need.

* *Uniforms.* Uniforms can be as simple as shorts and a T-shirt or a long-sleeved shirt. Some players like the protection of long sleeves—although warmer, sleeves ease the sting of the ball on the forearms. In beach volleyball, uniforms vary more widely. Swimsuits or athletic shorts and a short-sleeved or sleeveless shirt are appropriate. For playing outside, consider the weather conditions as you choose appropriate clothing. If you have any questions about uniforms, check with your organization.

* *Shoes.* A good shoe supports the arch and cushions the heel and ball of the foot. Volleyball or court shoes are fine for playing on hard courts. Running shoes aren't good, however, because they don't give lateral support. Volleyball shoes should be comfortable and broken in before they're worn during intense activity. Some players choose to wear shoes on grassy surfaces, while others prefer to play barefoot on the grass. Most beach players go barefoot or play with protective socks to avoid heat exposure or burning from the sand.

* *Knee pads.* Knee pads are typically worn for games played on hard surfaces. The use of knee pads on the beach and grass is not prohibited, but it's not as popular as on harder surfaces. Knee pads come in a variety of shapes and sizes, most of them made of foam or rubber covered with a soft elastic material. The pads should fit snugly and be comfortable for long periods. Because knee pads are designed to protect the knees, they make it a lot easier for young athletes to tolerate hitting the floor. If your local sporting goods store doesn't carry knee pads, you can order them through volleyball magazines or catalogs.

LEGEND FOR COURT DIAGRAMS

Player court positions (six on six)

RB = Right back
MB = Middle back
LB = Left back
RF = Right front
MF = Middle front
LF = Left front

Player roles (six on six or three on three)

P   = Passer
P1 = Primary passer
P2 = Second passer
S   = Setter
A   = Attacker
H   = Hitter
B   = Blocker
SR = Server
D   = Digger
T   = Tosser
C   = Coverer
🏐 = Position of the ball

For example, in a six-on-six game, an LB-P is a player in the left-back position who is acting as a passer and an RF-P/H is a player in the right-front position who is acting as a passer or hitter. In a three-on-three game, players are more flexible in terms of the court positions they cover, so we have just emphasized the roles they play. For example, a B player is prepared to block and a B/D player is prepared to block or dig; both players would move around the court as necessary.

Playing the Game of Volleyball

Although youth volleyball is played with two, three, four, or six players on a side, the most common format is to have three players and at least two substitutes. Nonstarter players will play just as much as the starters because everyone rotates in and out of the game, and no player specializes at any one position. Substitutions are unlimited, and each player who enters the game plays through three rotations before coming to the bench for a rest. When you progress to four versus four or the standard six-player game, there are limits on substitutions and how many times a player may enter the game. Encourage your league administrators to modify the substitution rules in six-on-six competition and on various playing surfaces to accommodate young performers and give them the opportunity to play in a competitive and fun environment.

Since the three-versus-three format is the most common in youth volleyball, we will focus on this format first. The basic concepts of the two-, three-, four-, and six-a-side games are similar, so we'll present information only about the three- and six-a-side games. If you play two- or four-a-side, you can easily adapt the material.

In three-a-side volleyball, the players position themselves so that one player is in the front half of the court (frontcourt) and the other two players split the back half (backcourt). In six-a-side volleyball, players are positioned similarly to cover the front- and backcourt areas. Figure 6.2 shows the comparison between the basic serve-receive positions used to start a game in both six-on-six and three-on-three volleyball.

The game starts as one team serves the ball over the net to the opponent. The opposing team tries to receive the serve by using a forearm pass to a setter (first contact), who sets to an attacker (second contact), who attempts to hit the ball into the opponent's court (third contact). Although it is not illegal for your players to hit the ball over the net on the first or second contact, players learn that controlling the three-hit combination allows their team to set the ball up for a more effective attack. After the serve players may move to any court position they wish, and play continues until either the ball hits the floor or a player on either team makes an error (i.e., hits the ball out of bounds or into the net). Players rotate one position clockwise when their team obtains the serve (except when they're receiving the serve for the *first* time in a match).

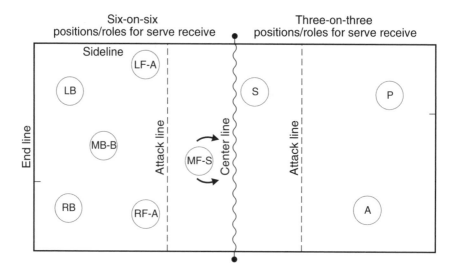

■ **Figure 6.2** Serve-receive positions for six-on-six and three-on-three volleyball.

In the standard six-player team game, play is initiated in the same manner as the three-on-three game. Players are not allowed the liberal movement on the court in the six-a-side game as they are in the three-a-side game. In the six-versus-six play, those in the back row can play any position there. Players in the front row can play any position in the front. Whereas there is no back-row attacking rule in the three-versus-three game, there are rules governing back row and front row attacking in the six-person teams.

Any player in the back row can attack the ball as long as he or she jumps from behind the 10-foot line (see figure 6.3). It is permissible to land in front of the 10-foot line after contacting the ball. Any player who jumps either on or in front of the 10-foot line is in violation of the back-row attack rule. The opponent would receive a point or side out, depending on who served the ball into play.

While moving to different positions in the front and back row is permissible, encourage your players to play all positions in both rows, so they develop a sense of how to play in each position. Rotating in the six-a-side game is quite simple. After getting the opportunity to serve, players from a team rotate clockwise one position and commence play (see figure 6.4). It is important that youngsters are aware of whom they are playing next to, which makes it easier to remain in the correct rotational order.

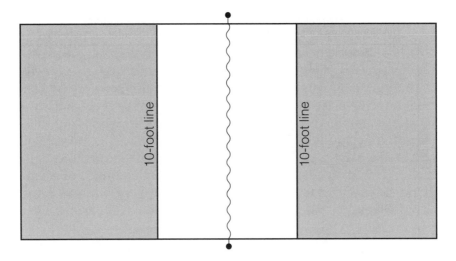

■ **Figure 6.3**   When attacking, back-row players must take off from somewhere in the shaded area (behind the 10-foot line).

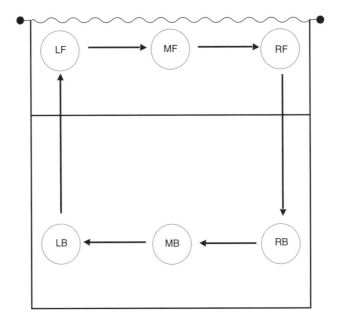

■ **Figure 6.4**   Rotational order for a six-a-side game.

Substitutions

Coaches should give everyone the opportunity to play; the substitutions are important to consider because they increase playing opportunities. In all forms of youth volleyball, various ways to substitute allow the players plenty of chances to improve their skills. The most common method is to allow a team member who is out to replace the person who has just rotated back to serve. This makes sense—the players understand when and whom to substitute, or go in, for. It virtually assures everyone equal playing time. Make sure at the end of each game, whether during practice or in a league game, that the same people do not begin the next game. This ensures equal playing time for all.

Another substitution method is to pair people in each position (two players are assigned to right back, two to left back, etc.) and split the game in half. If you're playing to 15 points, players come in to substitute for the partner when one team has reached 8 points. Remember to give each player the opportunity to start the game and to come in at the halfway point, so you ensure equal repetitions. Although winning is fun both for you and your athletes, it should take a back seat to everyone having the chance to practice and play the game.

In the six-a-side game, each team is allowed two time-outs per game. Time-outs last 30 seconds. While the substitution rules with the *traditional* six-player team games are relatively strict, be willing to modify these rules to ensure each player gets the opportunity to participate. You might have unlimited team substitutions for a team or individual or substitute for the player who is getting ready to serve, regardless of who that person is. Be sure to talk with your league administrators about the substitution rules you will be using. These administrators usually will be flexible in establishing rules that benefit all players, with more opportunities for playing time.

Player Positions

Before explaining player positions, we want to emphasize the importance of the role you play in helping your young athletes learn *all* the positions. Beginners should work on developing all the basic skills of volleyball without specializing in any one position. Many times, due to differences in physical, mental, or social maturity, young players are pushed into specialized roles (the tallest players are taught only to block and hit; the shortest players are expected only to pass and set) only to later find that other roles are more appropriate for them. All players must develop the fundamental skills of volleyball (serving, passing, setting, hitting, individual defense, and blocking) to play the game effectively. Give your players the opportunity to enhance their skills in competition and their lifetime enjoyment of the sport by assuring they each play all the positions.

To make court positioning easy for novice players to understand, show them the three different court positions for receiving a serve in volleyball with three-player and six-player teams (see figure 6.2). Since all players must be able to execute the basic skills of each position as they rotate and play each one, they will learn all aspects of the game.

Unit 7 will help you teach the skills required in each of the youth volleyball positions. The next section will describe the primary and secondary skill assignments for each position specific to youth volleyball, both in three-a-side and six-a-side volleyball.

Three-Player Volleyball Teams

Player A

Player A becomes a defensive player after initiating the serve. Player A is also one of the serve receivers in the back row. This player will become the secondary setter if Player B (the primary setter) receives the first ball over the net. Player A is in the first contact position (see figure 6.5).

Player B

Player B is the primary setter on offense and the primary blocker on defense. This player becomes the secondary attacker if Player C (the primary attacker) makes the second contact and must set for Player B. However, Player B should always strive to make the second contact (see figure 6.6).

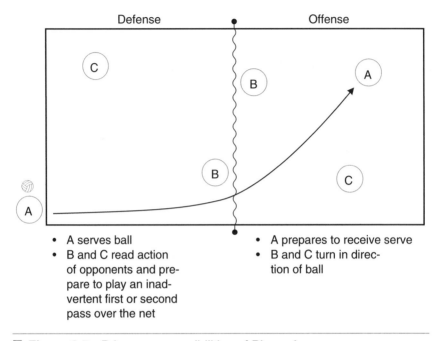

■ **Figure 6.5** Primary responsibilities of Player A.

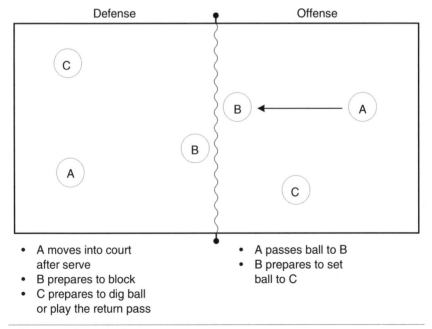

■ **Figure 6.6** Primary responsibilities of Player B.

Player C

Player C is the primary attacker on offense and primary digger on defense. This player will be the secondary digger or secondary setter if the served or attacked ball goes to Player A or B. Player C will take most of the third contacts (see figure 6.7).

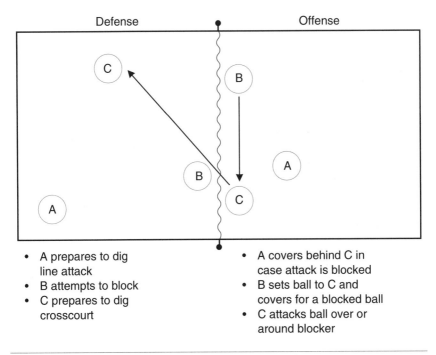

- A prepares to dig line attack
- B attempts to block
- C prepares to dig crosscourt

- A covers behind C in case attack is blocked
- B sets ball to C and covers for a blocked ball
- C attacks ball over or around blocker

Figure 6.7 Primary responsibilities of Player C.

Six-Player Volleyball Teams

In the six-player formation (see figure 6.2 on page 72) each player has specific responsibilities. Their roles and primary responsibilities are described here.

Right-Back and Left-Back Players

The right-back and left-back players will have primary serve-receive responsibility. Following serve reception, these players become concerned with covering any ball that might be blocked by the opponent. Assuming the ball crosses the net into the opponent's court and is kept in play by the opponent, they become defensive players.

Setter

The setter has primary responsibility for setting the second ball, allowing for an attack. The setter will primarily set to the left-front and right-front players. If the setter is unable to set the ball due to an errant pass, he or she is responsible for calling for help so that another player still can give a set.

Left-Front and Right-Front Players

The left-front and right-front players will be both the primary attackers on offense and important blockers on defense. They will be responsible for attacking the sets given by the setter and blocking attacks from the opponents. They will have very little responsibility in serve reception, unless you choose to modify serve-reception patterns to give them more responsibility.

Middle Blocker

The middle blocker will have primary defensive responsibility but not primary serve-reception responsibility. Once again, you may modify serve-reception patterns, if you wish, to include the middle blocker in the serve-reception line-up.

As players develop their skills, they'll become comfortable playing anywhere on the court. Try to be patient and supportive as your players learn the skills they need to play successfully in all positions. Young players need a solid base to gain confidence and enthusiasm for playing volleyball. As their coach, help them learn the skills and positions well. They'll be glad you did.

Scoring Points

Various scoring methods are used in volleyball. Depending on the type of competition, your team will use different scoring formats to speed up the game, keep tournaments on schedule, and give as many teams as possible an opportunity to play. In all these scoring methods, the team that commits an error (hitting the ball out-of-bounds, into the net, and so on) forfeits its opportunity to serve:

- *Standard-format scoring.* Games are played to 15 points, one point at a time. Only the serving team may score points, and a team must win by 2 points. A match consists of one team winning two of three games. Use this format when only two teams are competing and time is not a concern.

- *Rally scoring.* A point is scored on every serve, no matter which team served. The team who wins the point gets to serve the next point. For example, Team A serves the ball out-of-bounds; Team B gets the point and the next serve. This is a good format to use when time is limited. It is the only format in which the nonserving team can score points.

- *Timed games.* In large three-versus-three tournaments or round-robin competition, time is limited to keep the competition running smoothly. Depending on the number of teams and courts available, 8- to 10-minute games are typical times. Timed games may use standard-format or rally scoring.

Violations

Depending on the scoring system used, a team that commits one of the following errors usually is penalized by a point or *side out* (the serve goes to the opponent). The referee starts and stops the action and makes final decisions on all playing rules. Some leagues modify the rules for young players, so be sure to check with your league's administrators about whether these violations, or variations of them, will apply to your team:

- The ball hits the playing surface.
- The ball comes to rest (regardless of the skill being performed).
- The ball touches a player below the knee. (*Note:* This rule was recently modified. One modification considers illegal only *intentional* touches below the knee or waist, rather than any touch, intentional or not. The least restrictive modification is to allow any contact, regardless of body part. In fact, the Federation of

International Volleyball [FIVB], the international governing body for the sport, recently ruled that contact with any part of the body is legal. Be sure to ask your league director which ruling your league will be using.)

- A player touches the net.
- A player's foot completely crosses the center line, going on the other team's court. If any part of a player's body above the waist *touches* the opponent's court, that is also a violation.
- A player touches the ball twice in a row (consecutively). (An *exception*, however, is that in a block a player may block the spike and then contact the ball again before another teammate contacts it.)
- A team contacts the ball more than three times consecutively (except when blocking; see preceding point).
- A ball lands outside the court or touches an object outside the court.
- A player steps on the line when serving.
- A player attacks or blocks the ball when it is completely on the opponent's side of the net and before it has been contacted by the opposing team. (An attacker may contact the ball even if it is completely on the opponent's side of the net as long as the opposing team has made contact and as long as the attacker does not touch the net while attacking or blocking the ball. An attack or block is also allowed if any part of the ball is on the attacker's side of the net and if the attacker does not touch the net while contacting the ball.)

Referees

Most youth volleyball referees are volunteers, not professionals. As a volunteer, you surely understand and appreciate the difficult but important role referees play in youth sport. We hope you will remember this volunteer spirit as you react to a referee's decisions during a match. How you react when you think a referee has made a mistake is very important. Be a good role model for your players and their parents. If you think a rule was not properly enforced, raise the issue calmly or ask your floor captain to speak to the official for a clarification. It is *never* appropriate to scream or berate a referee's character during a match.

Remember, youth volleyball is for players to learn skills in a fun and motivating atmosphere. Do what you can to create this type of atmosphere as you coach and as you work with referees. Your players and their parents will learn a lot about being good sports by emulating your coaching behavior.

Referees enforce the rules of the game and they make sure players participate within the spirit of the rules. Players or coaches who commit any of the following actions may cause their team to be given an individual or team penalty:

- Making rude or vulgar remarks or gestures
- Engaging in disruptive or distracting behavior during the game from outside the court
- Yelling, shouting, or clapping at an opponent who is playing or attempting to play a ball

A referee may warn a coach or player (yellow card) about unsportsmanlike behavior. Referees may also penalize a coach or player (red card) by awarding the opponent a point or side out for continued inappropriate behavior. Finally, a referee may eject a coach or player from the court for excessive misconduct. See appendix C for a list of commonly used volleyball officiating signals.

If you would like more information on the game of volleyball or more specific rule interpretations, you can contact the following sources:

American Volleyball Coaches Association
1227 Lake Plaza Dr.
Colorado Springs, CO 80906
(719) 576-7777

National Association of Girls and Women in Sports
(NAGWS/AAHPERD)
1900 Association Dr.
Reston, VA 22091
(703) 476-3481

National Federation of State High School Associations
11724 NW Plaza Circle, P.O. Box 20626
Kansas City, MO 64195-0626
(816) 464-5400

USA Volleyball
3595 E. Fountain Blvd., Suite I-2
Colorado Springs, CO 80910-1740
(800) 275-8782

Unit 7

What Volleyball Skills and Drills Should I Teach?

In unit 4 you learned how to teach skills and to plan practices. This unit introduces you to the basic skills of volleyball and provides innovative drills and teaching ideas that will help you make this game come alive for your players.

Volleyball requires skills of mobility, balance, and jumping. This unit will help you guide beginners in developing these skills so they can enjoy playing at any level. We'll emphasize these five primary volleyball skills:

- *Serving*
- *Forearm passing*
- *Overhead passing (setting)*
- *Hitting*
- *Blocking*

With young, inexperienced players you'll have your work cut out for you. Emphasize proper mechanics, rather than outcomes, to give players a solid foundation on which to build. As you'll see, many volleyball skills complement each other in the learning process. We'll present ideas to help this learning progress smoothly and to add variety and fun to your practices. If you use these teaching tips, your players will learn the fundamentals while having a lot of fun.

How Do I Use Volleyball Drills Effectively?

Two simple coaching measures will improve the quality and effectiveness of your practices: teaching players to toss balls properly and to have success goals in mind for every drill. Once players can toss the ball properly, you'll have more time to coach and instruct. Taking time to teach beginners how to toss will be some of the best time ever spent. Helping players set goals for practices gives them something to strive for as they learn new skills. Players will be more motivated when they see the increasing success they are achieving in drills.

Tossing

Tossing is an important, yet often overlooked, part of running effective drills. The skill looks easier than it actually is. Teaching players how to toss will take some time, so be patient. Tossing the ball with no spin makes learning and performing other new skills much easier. Initially, you may have to do a lot of the tossing until your players are able to toss for each other. But once players learn to toss, they can run their own drills under your supervision.

With your feet shoulder-width apart, demonstrate a soft, two-handed toss from below the waist to a partner who catches it just above the head. Emphasize that there is no spin on the ball and the toss is high and soft. Have each player practice this with a partner who is about 10 feet away. It will take a lot of practice for them to toss softly and accurately, even to a partner who is stationary.

Setting Success Goals

Having fun is near the top of the goals list for most young volleyball players. And it should be a primary goal of yours as well.

But developing players' skills should be another major goal. You can support and monitor the improvement participants make by incorporating tangible measures of success into your practice drills. Establish an objective for each drill. Every objective should be realistic for the players' ages and skill levels. Here are some examples of goals a coach could set; you might select one of them to have your players achieve before rotating or moving on to another drill:

Jamie must hit 7 of 10 serves into the court before rotating.

Reggie will be able to set the ball to the target three times in a row.

A group of three must complete the pass, set, and spike sequence before rotating to the next drill station. The player who spikes the most balls into a specific area will have first chance at the water fountain!

Players have more enjoyment *and* improvement when they have something to aim for. Give them appropriate challenges to achieve success in practices and games—regardless of the score.

Serving

Besides putting the ball in play, the serve can be an effective way for a team to score points quickly. A good server can provide the momentum to boost his or her team to victory. Only the team that is serving (except in rally scoring) can score points. The server may choose to serve underhand or overhand. In youth volleyball, the server usually learns the underhand serve first.

Underhand Serve

The underhand serve allows beginning players to put the ball in play. It is easier to control than the overhand serve because it doesn't involve a toss. Here are some coaching points you should make as you introduce the skill.

FUNDAMENTALS OF UNDERHAND SERVING

1. Start with the weight on the back foot and the ball held in front of the toe by the "shelf" (nonhitting) hand (see figure 7.1a).
2. Keep the eyes focused on the ball until contact is made with the heel of the hand. Transfer weight from the back to the front foot as the arm swings to contact the ball (see figure 7.1b).
3. Drop the shelf hand and immediately hit the ball (see figure 7.1c).
4. Follow through with the hitting arm toward the top of the net. The hitting arm and back leg should be in line with the follow-through (see figure 7.1d).

■ **Figure 7.1** Fundamentals of underhand serving include (a) weight on the back foot, ball in front in the shelf hand; (b) arm swing to contact the ball; (c) drop the shelf hand and hit the ball; and (d) the follow-through.

================================= **Underhand Serve Drill** =================================

Name. Underhand Serve Drill

Purpose. To teach the mechanics of the underhand serve

Organization. Organize your players by lining up half of them along one end line and half of them along the other end line. Give a ball to each player on one side, and progress to the contact and follow-through as they aim to hit the serve. Repeat when each player on the other side has a ball.

Coaching Points. Ask the players if they hit the ball just as the shelf hand dropped. Also ask them if they transferred their weight through the serve.

Overhand Serve

The overhand serve is a bit more challenging for novice players because it requires being able to toss consistently. The overhand serve requires more coordination, timing, and strength, so teach it to players only after they have mastered the underhand serve. Many young players will doubt their ability to serve over the net with the overhand serve. A general test to see if they are indeed capable of serving over the net is to check if they can throw the ball over the net from the serving area. If they can throw over the net, most likely they can also serve overhand. The overhand serve, when mastered, is more versatile as it allows for greater speed, power, and control than the underhand serve.

Overhand Serve Toss

The toss is the key to a successful overhand serve. A ball tossed too high, too low, too far in front, or too far in back will cause the server to "chase" the toss and move out of proper precontact alignment. Servers should think of the ball as an extension of the shelf hand reaching up (see figure 7.2). Tell players to "lift" the ball above the shelf hand when

Figure 7.2 Overhand serve toss.

that arm is fully extended. The toss should always be in front of the hitting shoulder. Let players practice the whole skill of serving—but have them focus on the toss until it becomes consistent on each repetition. Here are some coaching points you should make as you introduce the skill.

FUNDAMENTALS OF OVERHAND SERVING

1. The body is pointed at the target area, and the weight is back on the opposite leg. The shelf hand holds the ball extended from the body at shoulder level in front of the hitting arm (see figure 7.3a).

2. The elbow of the hitting arm is about at ear level and a ball's radius away from the head of the server. The toss should be 12 to 18 inches above the shelf hand in front of the hitting shoulder (see figure 7.3b).

3. Weight transfers forward as the shoulders and hips come through and the player prepares to contact the ball (see figure 7.3c). Ask the players if contact was made before the shoulder and hips had swung through.

4. The heel of the hand should contact the ball with the arm fully extended and the wrist stiff (see figure 7.3d). The hand should contact directly at the center of the ball.

5. The hitting arm should swing fast, which will generate a quick and fluid motion with the server. Players who are having trouble serving over the net will improve if they swing fast.

6. On the follow-through, the hitting arm should follow behind the hitting-side leg. The arm must not cross in front of the body after making contact (see figure 7.3e).

■ **Figure 7.3** Fundamentals of overhand serving include (a) ball in the shelf hand, (b) the ball toss 12 to 18 inches above the shelf hand in front of the hitting shoulder, (c) shoulders and hips coming through, (d) heel of the hand contacting the ball, and (e) follow-through, hitting arm swinging through to hitting-side leg.

▰▰▰▰▰▰ **Overhand Serve Drills** ▰▰▰▰▰

Name. Shift and Contact Drill

Purpose. To teach players how to shift their weight forward and contact the serve in the middle of the ball

Organization. Have players pair up and line up 10 feet away from each other. Give each pair one ball and have them serve back and forth to each other. As the players serve, they should shift their weight and concentrate on preparing to make contact in the middle of the ball. Next, using the same format as they did in the underhand serve drill, have them practice serving over the net, tossing and hitting their serves in the middle of the ball. The players should begin midway between the attack line and end line, moving farther back as they become more proficient.

Coaching Points. Emphasize weight transfer and contact with the ball at the one o'clock position. Encourage low and consistent tosses off the hitting shoulder.

Error Detection and Correction for Overhand Serving

Players get frustrated when they cannot serve the ball into play consistently. Usually the toss is the problem in the overhand serve.

ERROR: The toss is inconsistent, which makes for an unreliable and uncontrolled serve.

CORRECTION
1. Check that the shelf hand is tossing the ball in front of the hitting shoulder.
2. Have players practice tossing without hitting the ball—to help them concentrate on tossing to the correct height (for the overhand serve, 12 to 18 inches from the shelf hand with the arm extended).
3. Make sure the server's feet are properly positioned.
4. The server should be making contact with the heel of the hand at the one o'clock position.
5. Remind the servers to swing their hitting arm as fast as they can.

Name. Picking Your Spot Drill

Purpose. To teach players how to control and direct their serves to specific areas on the court.

Organization. Players, each with a ball, line up on both sides of the net at midcourt, facing the net. The two groups take turns serving back and forth, serving to specific target areas designated by the coach (see the suggestions under Coaching Points). As the players achieve their goal of hitting the target area, they move five steps farther back toward the end line. As their skills develop, add other (towels or hoops) targets on the floor.

Coaching Points. Players should practice serving to the following areas on the court: short, deep, line, and cross (see figure 7.4). Your players may not be able to hit the targets, but serving *at* something will help them focus and concentrate.

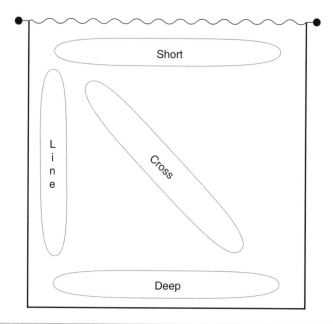

■ **Figure 7.4** Picking Your Spot Drill.

Forearm Passing

"Pass it over, Sterling!" "Great dig, Katie!" Whether it's used as a last-ditch effort to save an errant pass from going out of bounds or as a diving dig for an opponent's attack, the forearm pass helps make volleyball exciting. The forearm pass is for receiving serves and spikes, for digging balls that are no more than waist-high, and for playing any ball that has gone into the net. Any hard-driven spike or serve should be received with the forearm pass. Gaining control of the ball and accurately passing it to a teammate generates the offensive attack.

Beginning players usually feel comfortable contacting the ball off their forearms. Some will complain of a "sting" as the ball hits their arms. But as their technique improves, they won't be hitting or swinging at the ball; they'll learn to soften and direct the pass.

Ready Position for Forearm Passing

All players must be able to pass a serve or dig a spike with the forearm pass. The forearm pass begins with a good ready position. From there, players can execute the forearm pass and deliver the ball to the setter to begin the offense.

To learn the ready position for forearm passing, have your players stand with their feet shoulder-width apart, toes turned in slightly, and the right foot just slightly ahead of the left. As they bend at the waist and flex the knees, their weight should shift slightly forward onto the balls of the feet. Make sure that the head and shoulders are only slightly in front of the knees, and the arms are relaxed and extended in front of the body at a 45-degree angle. Have them keep the head up to follow the ball while keeping the knees bent and their weight over the balls of the feet (see figure 7.5).

■ **Figure 7.5**
Ready position for forearm passing.

Hand Position for the Forearm Pass

For the forearm pass, teach beginners to place their thumbs and palms facing close together. Figure 7.6 shows that when the thumbs and palms are together, an even platform is established. In all variations of the forearm pass the hand position is important to ensure a flat surface with the forearms.

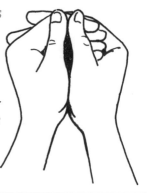

■ **Figure 7.6** Hand position for the forearm pass.

Platform Tilt

The platform tilt allows players to direct their passes to a target (see figure 7.7). When unable to face the target squarely, players can "dip" the shoulders and tilt the platform (the flat surface created by the forearms) to direct the ball accurately. The platform does not change (it remains flat), but the angle at which the ball hits and rebounds off the platform is adjusted to make the pass possible.

■ **Figure 7.7** Platform tilt.

FUNDAMENTALS OF FOREARM PASSING

1. Begin in a balanced ready position, with the arms relaxed but extended away from the body at about 45 degrees (see figure 7.8a).
2. Join the hands to form a flat surface with the forearms. The key is getting the thumbs together and pointed down toward the floor to form a flat forearm platform (see figure 7.8b).
3. Prior to contact, flex the legs. After contact, the arms follow through and direct the ball to the target (see figure 7.8c).

a   b   c

■ **Figure 7.8** Fundamentals of forearm passing include (a) arms relaxed and extended; (b) thumbs together, pointed downward; and (c) arms directing the ball to the target.

Error Detection and Correction for Forearm Passing

Young players often have a hard time judging speed and distance on a moving ball. They might overrun a ball or not even come close to making contact.

ERROR: A player misjudges and contacts the ball with either the hands or even the upper arms, instead of the forearms.

CORRECTION
1. Watch carefully as the player contacts the ball. Emphasize moving the feet first to get into a balanced position before contacting the ball.
2. The ball should contact the player above the wrist and below the elbow. A player can overcome misjudging the ball by tilting the forearm platform to deflect the ball toward the target.
3. Have the player establish a low position and extend the arms away from the body when contacting the ball.
4. Check the player at contact with the ball. A player's swinging the arms will cause the ball to rebound over the net or away from the target.

Forearm Passing Drills

Name. Triangle Passing Drill

Purpose. To teach players to pass at angles and use good communication skills

Organization. The players form a triangle (see figure 7.9). Player 1 tosses to Player 2, who uses a forearm pass to Player 3. Player 3 catches the ball and tosses back to Player 1, who uses a forearm pass to Player 2. The drill continues with the tosser saying, "Pass," the passer calling, "Mine," and the catcher answering, "Ready."

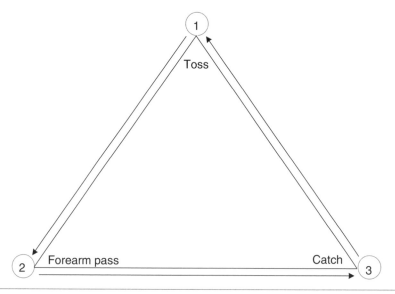

■ **Figure 7.9** Triangle Passing Drill.

Coaching Points. Remind players who are passing to square their hips to the ball, not to the target. They should stay low and tilt their platform to direct the ball to the target. Emphasize accuracy—meaning no catcher should have to move more than two steps.

Name. Hit the Setter Drill

Purpose. To teach players to forearm-pass the ball to the setter

Organization. The server (SR) tosses or serves the ball to the passer (P), who uses a forearm pass to the setter (S). The setter catches the ball and rolls it back to the server's position (see figure 7.10). The group rotates after 10 to 15 repetitions or after a specified time period. If players can serve overhand consistently, let them. Players having difficulty with serving overhand should toss overhand until they can serve consistently.

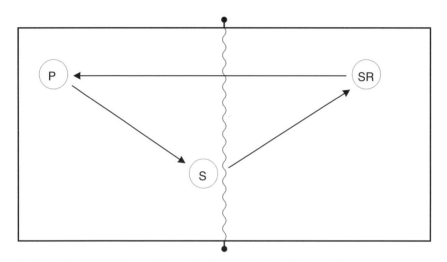

■ **Figure 7.10** Hit the Setter Drill (one passer).

Coaching Points. Reinforce the concepts of a ready position, platform, and tilt. Emphasize good communication. A good pass should be higher than the net and close enough to the setter that he or she can receive the ball with an overhead catch.

Variations. Using four players, the server (SR) tosses or serves underhand alternately to the two passers. The passers forearm-pass to the setter (S) (see figure 7.11). The setter stands inside a hula hoop. Have the primary passer (P1) or second passer (P2) pass so the setter can catch the ball without moving outside the hoop. Move the passers to different places on the court to help them learn how to "hit the setter" from different angles. The passer who is not receiving must turn and face the passer receiving the ball and stay in the ready position, ready to hustle after an errant pass.

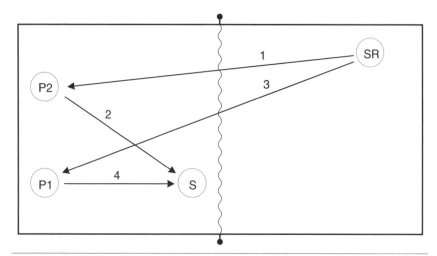

■ **Figure 7.11** Hit the Setter Drill (two passers).

Overhead Passing

The overhead pass is any pass contacted above the player's head. It may be used to play any ball that is moving high and slow (i.e., a *free ball*), to set up an attack (usually referred to as a *set*), or to keep the ball in play when a forearm pass or attack is not possible. The best-known overhead pass is the set, which is usually the second contact made in setting up an attack. The person directing the attack is called the setter, and the contact by the setter is called a set. The setter, who can see the entire court from the net, determines which hitter is in the best position for an attack. All players at one time or another—whether they play the setter or another position—will use the overhead pass to play the ball.

Beginning players are sometimes afraid of overhead passing with a hard ball. Consider using softer, lighter balls initially to teach the correct hand position. This way players won't worry about getting hit by the ball and can concentrate on learning the correct technique. As soon as they have gained some confidence, they can begin using a regular volleyball.

Ready Position for Overhead Passing

Teaching players to make an overhead pass from the correct ready position is the first part of developing successful overhead passing. Begin by having your players stand facing the left side of the court with their feet shoulder-width apart, the right foot slightly ahead of the left. The knees should be bent slightly, and the weight should be on the balls of the feet. In this semicrouched position, the players will raise and cup their hands above the forehead, waiting for the ball (see figure 7.12).

■ **Figure 7.12** Ready position for overhead passing.

Hand Position for Overhead Passing

Players should shape their hands like the volleyball itself, in front of the forehead and set to locate the ball through the "window" formed by the thumbs and forefingers. The wrists are cocked back and the fingers are spread and relaxed, four to eight inches from the forehead, as if holding a volleyball (see figure 7.13).

■ **Figure 7.13** Hand position for overhead passing.

FUNDAMENTALS OF OVERHEAD PASSING

1. In the ready position for overhead passing, the feet are staggered (the right foot slightly ahead of the left). The weight is on the balls of the feet. The hands are shaped like the ball, above the forehead, locating the ball (see figure 7.14a).

2. Contact the ball in the middle of the forehead (see figure 7.14b).

3. The pads of the fingers, not the palm, should contact the ball (see figure 7.14c).

4. Whenever possible, players should square their shoulders to the target. As contact is made, the player extends the arms and legs up (see figure 7.14d).

a   b   c   d

■ **Figure 7.14** Fundamentals of overhead passing include (a) ready position, (b) ball contacted as it is in line with the middle of the forehead, (c) pads of the fingers contacting the ball, and (d) the arms and legs extending at contact.

Overhead Passing Drills

Name.   Triangle Overhead Passing Drill

Purpose.   To teach players the fundamentals of overhead passing

Organization.   Arrange the players in sets of triangles (as in the forearm passing drills). Player 1 tosses to Player 2, who overhead-passes the ball to Player 3. Player 3 catches the ball and tosses to Player 1, who overhead-passes to Player 2. Player 2 catches the ball, and the drill continues. The tosser should say, "Pass," the passer calls, "Mine," and the catcher responds, "Ready." Have the players complete five movements of the ball around the triangle, with the players who receive the ball beating the ball into position, taking not more than two steps.

Coaching Points.   Emphasize good, accurate tossing in this drill. A good overhead pass is more likely with a good toss or pass.

Variations.   In the same arrangement, the players start with a toss and then overhead-pass continuously, reversing direction on the coach's command. With four players, each player overhead-passes, moves quickly to the next spot on the floor, reestablishes position, and prepares to overhead-pass another ball (see figure 7.15).

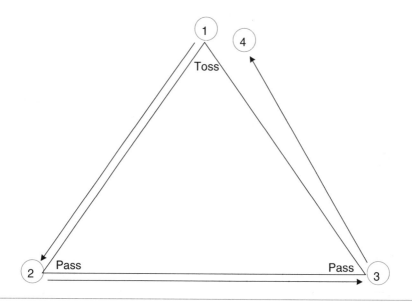

■ **Figure 7.15**   Triangle Overhead Passing Drill (four-player variation).

The fourth player starts in the corner where the ball begins. As Player 1 tosses to Player 2, Player 1 follows the toss and steps into Player 2's spot as Player 2 overhead-passes to Player 3. Player 2 follows the pass to Player 3, and Player 3 then overhead-passes to where Player 4 has stepped in for Player 1. As your players improve their skills, you may add a forearm pass to the second contact.

Name. Free-Ball Overhead Passing Drill

Purpose. To develop the overhead passing skills to handle a free ball (first contact) and overhead passing (second contact) situation

Organization. The server (SR) begins by tossing the ball over the net to the passer (P), who passes to the setter (S). The setter sets the ball parallel to the net to the passer, who moves up to within three feet of the net to catch the set and then rolls the ball back to the server (see figure 7.16).

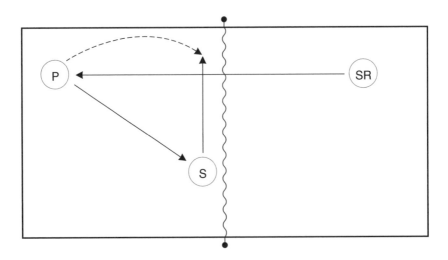

■ **Figure 7.16** Free-Ball Overhead Passing Drill.

Coaching Points. The toss represents how a free ball (any easy, lofty return) would come back over the net. The passer and the setter work to make each other's tasks as easy as possible by using high, accurate passes and sets to each other.

Variations. Using the same setup, the passer forearm-passes to the setter, and the setter sets the ball parallel to the net to the passer. Move the passer to different free-ball receiving positions, and vary the angle at which the passer must pass to the setter.

Error Detection and Correction for Overhead Passing

Beginning players are sometimes afraid of injuring their fingers from overhead passing. Using softer, lighter balls, beginners can learn the feel of overhead passing on the hands.

ERROR: Players who are nervous about a hard contact use an improper hand position for overhead passing.

CORRECTION
1. Begin teaching overhead passing with lighter balls so these players are not afraid of contact.
2. Review the fundamentals of hand position; have the players toss and pass back and forth with partners to get used to the feel of the volleyball falling from above.

Hitting

Pass, set, spike! Spiking a ball is one of the most thrilling plays—at all levels. Once your players have the skills to set up a teammate for an attack (spike), they will enjoy the excitement that great team play generates.

The *attack* is a general term used to describe how the ball is played over the net. *Spiking* is the primary skill used to attack the ball, and it is usually the third contact in the three-contact offense. A team that develops a strong attack will have opportunities to score points more readily.

Ready Position for Hitting

The ready position for an attack approach is slightly different from other ready positions. The spiker must turn and run back several steps from the net to have room for an approach to hit the ball explosively. The attacker should be standing in a relaxed position with arms comfortably at the sides. He or she should be at the side of the court, about 8 to 12 feet back off the net, waiting for the set (see figure 7.17).

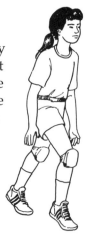

■ **Figure 7.17** Ready position for the attack (hit).

FUNDAMENTALS OF ATTACKING: THE APPROACH

1. The most common attack approach is a four-step pattern. Left-handed players start step 1 with the left foot; right-handers begin with the right foot. A player needs an explosive movement from step 2 to step 3 to set up the quick foot plant into the jump (see figure 7.18, a-d).
2. The arms extend and swing straight back, as high as possible on the third step. As the fourth (closure) step begins, the arms drive forward in a full sweeping motion to help drive the player off the ground to attack the ball (see figure 7.18, e and f).

■ **Figure 7.18**   Fundamentals of the attack approach include (a-d) four-step approach footwork, (e) arms swinging back on the third step, and (f) arms coming forward, driving the player up off the ground.

FUNDAMENTALS OF ATTACKING: BODY POSITION AND CONTACT

1. In contacting the ball, think of the arm as a whip and the hand as the tip of that whip. The snap of the whip begins in the shoulder. The elbow of the hitting hand should be drawn back, high and away from the shoulder (see figure 7.19a).
2. As contact is made, the hand should be firm and open, hitting the top half of the ball with the palm. Contact the ball at the one to two o'clock position (see figure 7.19b).
3. Follow through quickly. In the follow-through the arm should remain on the same side of the body (not crossing over the body), finishing behind the hitting-side leg.
4. Remind your players that they will get a penalty for touching the net with any part of the body.

a   b

■ **Figure 7.19** Fundamentals of the attack contact include (a) the elbow of the hitting hand drawn back and (b) the open hand contacting the ball at the one o'clock position.

There are different ways to attack the ball. Each can be effective in scoring points. Usually, the harder the ball is hit, the less time opponents have to dig the attack. However, teams can use other types of attacks with great success to keep opponents off balance. These attacks are used in various game situations:

- *Hard-driven spike*—A ball hit forcefully down into the opponent's court.

- *Off-speed spike*—A controlled placement of the ball to an open space. This attack is used when a block is present and the hitter can see that an open area around or behind the block is not being defended. The attacker may take a full swing, but then let up and hit the ball softly to an open area.

- *Down ball*—An attack used from a standing position to place the ball into the opponent's court. A player who doesn't have time for an approach or jump can hit the down ball.

- *Tip*—An open-handed placement of the ball made with the pads of the fingers. An attacker uses a tip when he or she sees an opportunity to place the ball in an open area and is not able to swing fully. Remind players that they may not hold, grasp, or throw the ball when tipping.

Attack Drills

Name.   Arm-Swing Attack Drill

Purpose.   To help players develop the proper arm swing and contact point for spiking

Organization.   A player (who has learned how to toss) stands in the setter's position. The player tosses high sets to attackers who are 8 to 10 feet from the net, a distance that isn't intimidating to the young players. The attackers approach and work on the mechanics of the approach and arm swing.

Coaching Points.   Instruct players to concentrate on contacting the ball high (at the one o'clock position) and following through quickly. Emphasize getting the hitting-side elbow high (at shoulder height) and away from the body as they prepare to hit.

Error Detection and Correction for Attacking

Timing is critical in attacking a set. Young players often forget the approach, jump too soon or too late, and then have problems hitting accurately when they get into the air.

ERROR: A player repeatedly hits the ball out-of-bounds or into the net. The player seems to lack body control.

CORRECTION
1. The player must contact the ball at the peak of the jump.
2. Check the approach and timing of the jump. Walk through the approach with your player. Remind him or her to watch the set to be able to judge when to approach for the hit.
3. Have each player show you her or his arm swing from a standing position. Check that the elbow is away from the body and the *palm* of the hand is making good, solid contact on the ball.
4. Emphasize speed over accuracy in the player's approach and arm swing. A player who both approaches and swings quickly will feel confident of learning the skill of attacking, even if the ball travels far out of the playing area.

Name. Line Pepper Drill

Purpose. To develop the proper arm swing and contact point for an off-speed hit from a tossed or passed ball

Organization. Three players stand in a line. The middle one, a tosser (T), has a ball (see figure 7.20). The tosser begins by tossing a high, soft ball to an attacker (A), then steps aside to allow the drill to continue. The attacker then makes a standing, off-speed hit across to the digger (D). The digger must dig (retrieve) the attacker's spike and try to target the dig for the tosser, who reenters the drill to catch the dig from the digger. They then rotate positions.

Coaching Points. The tosser must toss the ball high enough for the attacker to hit. The attacker's hit must be accurate enough for the digger to dig the pass back to the tosser. The catcher wants to be to the right of the digger, since this is the direction that most diggers will want to dig in a game.

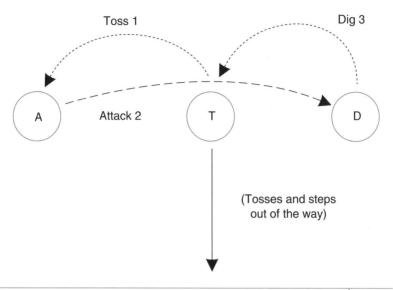

■ **Figure 7.20** Line Pepper Drill.

Name. Two-Player Jumping Spike Drill

Purpose. To develop the players' abilities to attack the ball with an approach jump

Organization. Players form pairs; each pair should have a ball. From the overhead passing position, one player sets (from a toss) the ball about 15 feet high and 2 to 4 feet off the net. The partner, concentrating on timing and the approach, attacks the toss and hits it in the opposite court. Each player hits 10 spikes before rotating positions with the partner.

Coaching Points. Emphasize using proper footwork and speed in the approach, exploding upward, and trying to hit the ball at the peak of the jump. You can make this drill competitive by awarding a point for every hard-driven spike into the court, no points for a tip, and subtracting a point for every ball hit into the net or out-of-bounds.

Name. Attack Recovery Drill

Purpose. To help players develop timing for the approach jump and to combine two skills in sequence (the pass and the spike)

Organization. Use two to four balls in each court. The server (SR) tosses or serves to the passer/attacker (P/A). The passer/attacker overhead-passes balls that are high and slow or forearm-passes balls that are low and fast to the setter (S). The setter sets balls that are high and slow or forearm-passes balls that are low and fast to the passer/attacker. The passer/attacker approaches the net and jumps to attack the ball into the opposite court (see figure 7.21). The passer/attacker retrieves her or his own attack and moves to the serving position. The server becomes the setter and the setter moves to the passer/attacker position.

Coaching Points. If the timing of this drill is too difficult, have the passer/attacker perform a standing spike.

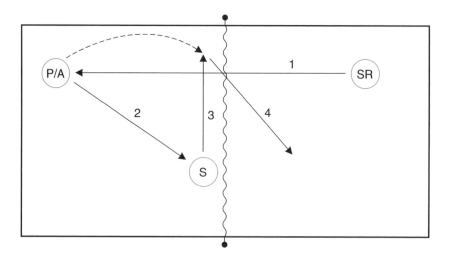

■ **Figure 7.21** Attack Recovery Drill.

Blocking

Good blocking involves ability in timing and in reading the offensive hitter's intentions. As you introduce blocking to your team, emphasize that every member, short or tall, can play an effective role as a blocker. Although taller players have an advantage, shorter players also can block to deflect and slow down hard-driven spikes.

The objective in blocking is to block a hard-driven spike back into the opponent's court or to deflect it high into the air on the blocker's side of the court. Without the block, an offensive team's spike very likely will earn a point or a side out. In youth volleyball with a smaller court and fewer players, blocking is limited to one blocker and some simple footwork.

Ready Position for Blocking

The ready position gets your players aligned to set a good block. Begin by teaching your players to stand facing the net with their hands held shoulder-width apart at head level. The hands should be open, with the fingers spread and the palms facing the net. The knees are slightly bent, and the weight is on the balls of the feet. Players will move in this coiled position, ready to spring up to block an opponent's attack (see figure 7.22).

■ **Figure 7.22**   Ready position for blocking.

Hand Position for Blocking

As the blocker jumps to block, the hands should surround and smother the ball (see figure 7.23). The blocker's fingers are spread and angled to deflect the ball toward the floor. The hands do not wave or flail at the ball. A blocker who is short, is a weak jumper, or is late jumping to block may perform a *soft block* (see figure 7.24).

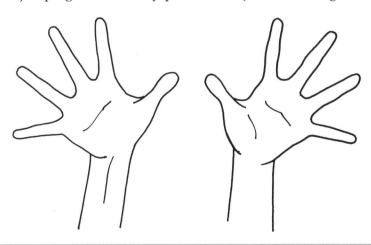

■ **Figure 7.23**   Hand position for blocking.

■ **Figure 7.24** Hand position for soft blocking.

The blocker's fingers are still spread, but the hands are angled backward toward the blocker's court. The soft block merely deflects the ball back into the blocker's court to be played by teammates. The rules allow the blocker's team to make three more contacts if a soft block is deflected and playable.

Footwork for Blocking

A blocker moving along the net uses a step-close-step footwork pattern to get into position across from the hitter. From the semi-crouched, ready position for blocking (see figure 7.25a), the player steps first with the leg closer to the direction in which she or he intends to move (see figure 7.25b). Next, the blocker closes the feet together by pushing off the trailing foot. The feet do not cross. The player is now ready to explode up to block the attack (see figure 7.25c). This step-close-step footwork helps players control momentum and maintain balance as they block.

■ **Figure 7.25**   Step-close-step blocking footwork.

FUNDAMENTALS OF BLOCKING

1. The blocker should face the net with legs slightly bent and with the weight on the balls of the feet. Hands are open and relaxed, held in front of the shoulders at head-level (see figure 7.26a).
2. As the attacker goes up to hit, the blocker watches the hitter and explodes up from the coiled position with both arms and hands extended to block the ball back into the opponent's court (see figure 7.26b).
3. Emphasize that players should stay away from the net and off the center line. Players should land on both feet and be ready to move in any direction after blocking (see figure 7.26c).
4. In most cases, the blocker should jump *after* the attacker, since the attacker must swing at the ball after jumping.

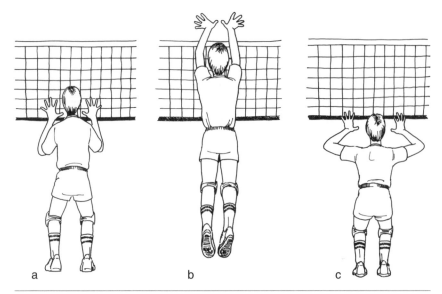

■ **Figure 7.26** Fundamentals of blocking include (a) the ready position, (b) both arms and hands extending to block the ball, and (c) the player landing on both feet, ready to move in any direction after blocking.

Drills for Blocking

Name. Slide Drill

Purpose. To reinforce proper lateral movement in a coiled position for blocking

Organization. Two players stand on chairs about 10 feet apart, each holding a volleyball just above net level. Each holds the ball on his or her own side of the net, facing the net and the blocker. A third player, the blocker, jumps and blocks (makes contact with) the first volleyball, lands, and moves into a coiled ready position (using the step-close-step lateral footwork) to block the other volleyball being held. The player goes back and forth using the step-close-step footwork and jumps to block (contact) the balls being held by the players on the chairs.

Coaching Points. Make sure the blocking players move with their hands at head level, with their eyes on the imaginary hitter, and from a coiled position.

Variations. After the blocker lands from a block, have the players on the chairs toss a ball in a high arch to each other. Challenge the blocker to get to the spot where the ball is being tossed before it is caught.

Name.   Player Versus Coach Blocking Drill

Purpose.   To teach players what a hard-driven spike feels like when blocking

Organization.   The coach plays on one side of the net, and the team members on the other. With the net lowered so players can get their hands above it, the coach tosses to herself and spikes the ball at the outstretched blocker's hands. Players earn a point for either blocking the ball back into the coach's court or making a soft block back into the blocker's court. They lose a point if the ball goes out-of-bounds or into the net. Coaches should attack the ball with the same power as their players would face in practice and competition.

Coaching Points.   As the strength and skills of your players develop, use a higher net and have them jump to block the attack.

Error Detection and Correction for Blocking

Blockers often have a hard time keeping their hands firm and angled properly. When a blocker's hands are not properly positioned, an attacker will be able to hit balls off the block and out of play.

ERROR: Hard-driven and off-speed attacks are deflecting off the blocker and out-of-bounds.

CORRECTION
1. The blocker must keep his or her body parallel to the net, with the hands extended above the net if possible, facing the court.
2. The blocker should turn the outside hand in toward the court so the ball will rebound back into the attacker's court.
3. The blocker should keep the hands firm and strong, angled for a deflection to rebound directly down (unless the blocker is executing a soft block).
4. The blocker should jump after the attacker has jumped, which gives a greater chance for the ball to be blocked.

Name.   Form Blocking Drill

Purpose.   To develop the blocker's timing with the set and the attack

Organization.   The Passer (P) tosses to the setter (S), who sets to the attacker (A) (see figure 7.27). Then the attacker approaches to spike. When the setter contacts the ball, the blocker (B) moves to block the attack with a step-close-step footwork pattern. The blocker moves back and forth with each toss to the setter. The blocker gets 2 points for every block into the opponent's court and 1 point for every soft block back into the blocker's court. The blocker must get 5 points before the players rotate positions.

Coaching Points.   You may add a server on the blocker's side of the court to make the drill more game-like. Make sure you don't rush beginning players into variations while they're struggling with footwork and technique. Extra directions and variations will only frustrate them more.

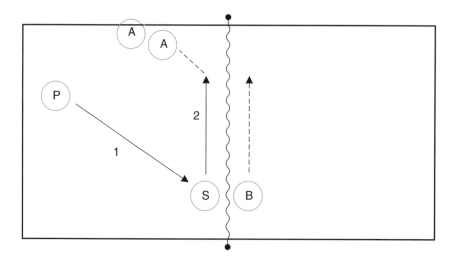

■ **Figure 7.27**   Form Blocking Drill.

Name. Triangle Blocking Game

Purpose. To help players develop timing for blocking the attack from various areas on the court

Organization. Two three-player teams are on opposite sides of the net (see figure 7.28). A server (SR) serves to either the passer (P) or to the passer/attacker (P/A), who passes to the setter (S). The setter sets to the passer/attacker, who approaches and attacks the ball. The blocker (B) attempts to block the attack. The attacking team earns a point by hitting a spike into the opponent's court. The blocking team earns a point for a soft block into its own court or a block back into the opponent's court. If a ball is hit out-of-bounds by an attacker or is blocked into the net or out of play, the team loses a point. Play stops after each attack and block, players rotate, and teams switch serving. The game is played to 7 or more points, depending on the players' abilities.

Coaching Points. A soft block is effective as long as the ball stays in play. Not all attacks can be blocked directly to the opponent's floor. A controlled soft block is better than no block at all.

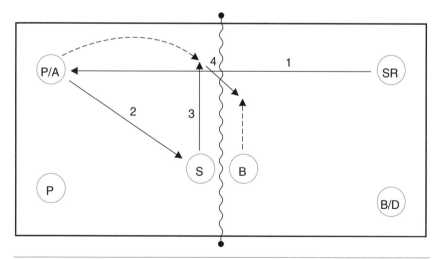

■ **Figure 7.28** Triangle Blocking Game.

Unit 8

How Do I Get My Players to Play as a Team?

Developing individual skills is important, but getting your players to work together and play as a team may be even more of a challenge. Do your players recognize when to join together to block the opponent's attack? Do they try to combine the skills of the game (passing, setting, hitting, etc.) or do they just try to "get it over"?

Helping players improve their individual skills is only the start. To develop team players, you must help them learn to also make good decisions on the court.

Good progressions in drills and practice games allow players to develop their team decision-making skills. These situations are competitive, yet not overwhelming. Players learn team concepts best when the practice atmosphere is both fun and challenging. So don't rush players into competition too soon. They'll let you know when they're ready.

In this unit, you'll learn how to work with your players in developing their team play. We'll explain how to use the skills described in unit 7 to build your team's framework for competition. Remember TEAM as a password to making a cohesive *team*:

> T—*Tactics*: working toward a common goal
>
> E—*Essentials*: developing skills
>
> A—*Attitude*: assisting teammates
>
> M—*Membership*: helping each player feel like part of the team

What About the Team on Offense?

An accurate pass to the setter, a well-executed set, and a hard-driven attack are keys to success in offensive volleyball. After passing the serve (or the opponent's attack), the offense begins with a set to a hitter and an attack over the net. Teams that can control the ball through passing, setting, and hitting will reduce the number of errors and have better chances to score points and maintain the serve.

But the offense can't start until the team plays solid defense and passes an opponent's serve or digs an opponent's spike. And serve reception and digging—two skills of defensive transition—are essential to enabling the offense to develop. Later in this unit, we will cover defense and defensive transition skills. Before that discussion we will describe a team's offense once the ball has been passed or dug up after the opponent's serve or attack.

Offensive Alignments

After your team has successfully received a serve or volley from the opponent, it assumes the offense. When your team takes the offense, its members will be working to set up a well-placed or hard-driven spike back over the net. In the following sections you'll see how to align your team's offense to fit the type of defense it faces.

If the opponents are blocking your attack, your players should cover any possible tips or deflections. If no block is present, your offensive alignment will change to prepare for the defensive transition. The next sections describe the player alignments (which work on any playing surface) for either situation: with or without a block.

Error Detection and Correction for Team Offense

Sometimes players are unsure of their positions on the court and don't know who should play a ball hit between two players.

ERROR: Players stand around without communicating to each other when a ball comes between them. Attacks or serves hit the floor, and the players blame one another for not playing the ball.

CORRECTION

1. Players should always be in a flexed ready position, prepared to go after a ball hit in their direction.
2. Players who can play the ball while moving in the direction of the target have priority in playing it.
3. Players should turn to watch their teammates hit the ball and should be ready to play an errant pass.
4. Players should practice calling, "Mine" or "I" any time the ball is hit to them.

Three-Player Offensive Alignments

Most youth volleyball games and practices will have three players on each side. Even if your team plays in a six-on-six league, practicing three-on-three will give your players more opportunities for ball contact and skill learning. We will first discuss how to align your players for the offense in simpler situations of three-on-three and then give the adjustments for the more traditional six-on-six games.

Offensive alignment without a blocker. Your team can take advantage of an opposing team that does not put a blocker up at the net, thus defending against the opponent's immediate return. As figure 8.1 shows, the passer (P) first passes to the setter (S). The hitter (H) is in the hitting position, awaiting the setter's set. As the hitter attempts to attack the set from the setter, the setter may step off the net and prepare for the opponent's return. After passing to the setter, the passer looks to see if the hitter has a blocker and then prepares to assist in the event of the opponent's return when the hitter hits the offensive attack. If the hitter *passes* the first ball, the setter will still set, and the passer can assume the hitting role on the third (next) contact.

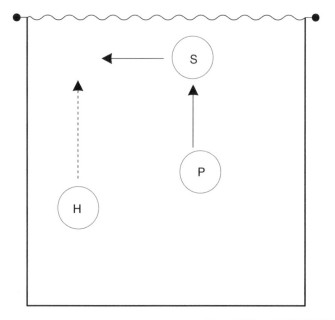

■ **Figure 8.1** Three-on-three offensive alignment without a blocker.

Offensive alignment with a blocker.   With a blocker in place against your offensive alignment, you should make minor adjustments to provide coverage against a block that may deflect back into your court. If your hitter (H) faces a blocker when going for the hit, the passer (P) and the setter (S) should move in closer to the hitter to cover the ball that the opponent blocks (see figure 8.2).

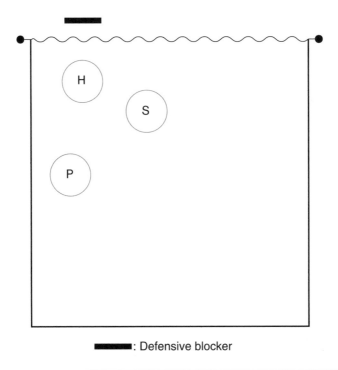

■■■■■: Defensive blocker

■ **Figure 8.2**   Three-on-three offensive alignment with a blocker.

Players must learn to see if the other team has a blocker at the net. In coaching, emphasize the importance of team members communicating with one another as they move into position and set the ball up for the hitter at the net. The teammates who are covering the hitter should be in a low and balanced position, ready to pursue the ball in any direction. Although making the adjustment for a blocker at the net is not difficult, it is essential to an effective offense.

Six-Player Offensive Alignments

Offensive alignments in six-on-six volleyball are more complex because more players are on the court. Every one of these players must understand their personal responsibilities on the court as well as what responsibilities their teammates hold. Figures 8.3a and 8.3b illustrate coverage positions for all six players. Emphasize to your players that although these alignments are not always possible, they are desirable. If players cannot get to these positions (as shown in figures 8.3a and 8.3b), they should stop as soon as the attacker makes the contact, and anticipate a ball deflecting off the opponent's block. The players closest to the attacker probably will have the most opportunities to respond to a blocked ball, but the players who are farther away must also be ready for and alert to balls deflected deep into the court.

Offensive alignment without a blocker. If the opponent chooses not to block, the alignment for a six-player offense will be similar to the three-person format. Assuming the opponents dig the attack, the players with defensive responsibility can "cheat" their way back to their defensive positions with little threat of their teammate's attack getting blocked. In the six-player game the setter will be played by the middle-front player, eliminating confusion as to who should set the attacker and allowing the other players to focus on their individual areas of responsibility.

Offensive alignment with a blocker. Whether your opponents use one or two blockers, you'll need to adjust your strategy. The likelihood of your team's attack getting blocked has increased, and all players should share the responsibility of covering the ball when the block occurs. Most balls are blocked in front of the 10-foot line, so your alignment should protect that immediate area around the attacker. If the *left-front attacker* receives the set, the setter and left back will share equal responsibility in picking up the ball blocked 10 feet or closer to the net. If the *right-front player* receives the set, then the setter and right back will have primary responsibility.

It is critical that all other players assume positions to protect the majority of the court, defending against balls that land elsewhere. A basic rule in covering the court is that a backcourt defender should never be directly behind or beside a teammate. By following this rule, the court will be balanced in terms of defensive coverage.

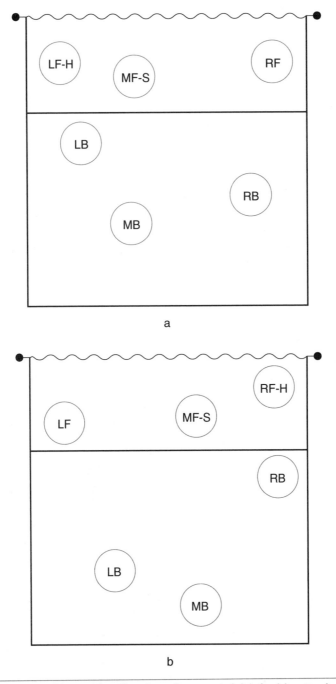

Offensive Skill Progressions

Lead-up progressions give players chances to practice their skills in small but competitive doses. Your players will need some lead-up drills to help them develop the team concept. Beginning-level volleyball skill progressions will give you some ideas for later practice games. These skill progressions work well with the youngest volleyball players—ages five to eight. You'll find practice plans in appendix B that you can modify to incorporate the lead-up skill progressions appropriately into your program.

All progressions begin with a toss and catch, using familiar skills. After players fully understand the basic movements and sequence of three contacts, you can have them use balloons and foam balls to develop their continuous volleying. Through these progressions your players can develop their

- agility and judgment in moving to the ball;
- correct positioning under the ball;
- understanding of rules, court positions, and player responsibilities; and
- experience in how a team plays together on offense.

Be creative in modifying these progressions to match your players' experience and abilities. If players are afraid to make contact with the ball in an overhead pass, for example, let them practice with softer balls until they develop the skills and confidence they'll need for advanced progressions. Remember, helping your players learn the basic skills is one of the most important things you'll be doing as their coach. They won't always be patient as you emphasize the basics. Most players would rather "just play." By providing drills and lead-up games for your players, they can enjoy playing plus have plenty of opportunities to improve their skills and knowledge of volleyball.

The drills you'll find here are appropriate for both the three-on-three and six-on-six games. They simply break down the six-player team into smaller parts that younger performers can understand. When you progress to six-player teams with your young players, be sure they recognize that they have already been playing this game for a long time in groups of three. This will make them confident as they first play six versus six.

▰▰ Beginning-Level Volleyball Skill Progressions ▰▰

Name.   Toss-and-Set Volleyball

Purpose.   To help players judge and move to the ball

Organization.   Have players get in groups of three, giving each group a ball. One player will toss the ball to the other player, who will set it to the target, who is the third player. This player will then toss it back to the first player.

Coaching Points.   Encourage players to anticipate where the ball is going and then move to that spot for the set before the ball gets there.

Variations.   Instead of catching and tossing, have two passers communicate and overhead pass the last toss over the net. The tosser should toss *away* from the setter who consequently will have to incorporate movement into the drill.

Offensive Lead-Up Games

Lead-up games allow players to experience what it is like to use their skills as a team while competing against another team. As players are learning skills, they need time to practice and gain confidence in their abilities. Lead-up games let players try out their new skills in a safe, nonthreatening environment.

▰▰ Offensive Lead-Up Games ▰▰

Name.   Ball Over the Line (Catch and Toss)

Purpose.   To help players learn how to move to the ball and work as a team to generate an offensive attack

Organization.   Set up three versus three on a youth volleyball court without a net. One player begins with an underhand toss over the center line (serve). The receiving team communicates, deciding who will catch it; the player who does then tosses (passes) to a second teammate. The second team member moves to catch the pass and then overhead-tosses to the third teammate, who catches and tosses the ball into an open space on the opposite court (attack). If the ball hits the floor or goes out-of-bounds, the opposite team gets a point (see rally scoring, p. 79), regardless of who started the toss (serve). Play for a set time or until a team accumulates a certain number of points.

Coaching Points. Encourage players to catch with two hands above their foreheads as they move under the toss and position their bodies to make a safe catch. Each toss should be at least head high. Give positive feedback or points when players talk and call "Mine." Communication is a big part of playing team offense. This game can be adapted for six-player teams, and it is a valuable way to teach youngsters movement and communication skills. Remind the players to keep the catch and throw at game speed, to be as close as possible to a real game.

Name. Ball Over the Net (Catch and Toss)

Purpose. To help players learn about team offense without the pressure of performing all the skills

Organization. Set up for three versus three or four versus four on a youth volleyball court with a net 6 feet 1 inch high. Play begins with a toss over the net to the opponent. The receiving team makes a two-handed, overhand catch. After catching the toss, the player extends, pushing the ball from his or her forehead to set to the next teammate. On the third contact, the player may run or jump with the ball and attack, either throwing or hitting it over the net. Three contacts are required on each side by at least two players before the team returns the ball over the net. A team can score only when it has made the first toss or serve and the opponents have made a mistake (standard scoring). If the team tossing first makes an error (hitting the ball into the net or out-of-bounds), it doesn't lose any points, but the other team gets the serve.

Coaching Points. Encourage players to hit or throw the ball into open areas of the court.

Name. Rotation Lead-Up Game

Purpose. To encourage players to perform skillfully in the receiving, setting, and attacking positions

Organization. Set up for three versus three, four versus four, or six versus six on a youth volleyball court. One team begins by serving or tossing over the net. Each team attempts to make three contacts on its side of the net (preferably, a pass, set, and spike).

Play continues until the volley ends. Teams can rotate only after they have made three contacts. Each team earns a point when it makes three contacts on a side. If the ball is returned over the net on an errant first or second contact, the game continues but no point is awarded. Teams alternate serving after each rotation or side out.

Coaching Points. Reinforce players in their efforts to achieve the three-contact offensive sequence (pass, set, hit). Even if their skills are still unpolished, they'll be learning team concepts.

Name. Single Skills Game

Purpose. To emphasize the importance of single skills (passing, setting) within a team

Organization. Set up for three versus three or four versus four on a youth volleyball court. You'll want to avoid six on six with this game since the opportunities to learn these individual skills decrease as you add more players. Teams play three-contact volleyball, using only one skill (a forearm or overhead pass) to play the ball. For example, one team may use the overhead pass exclusively, while its opponent uses only the forearm pass. The coach indicates when it's time to change skills, or a coach and assistant can stand at the end lines and flash signs to the opposite team showing what skills they are to use (see figure 8.4).

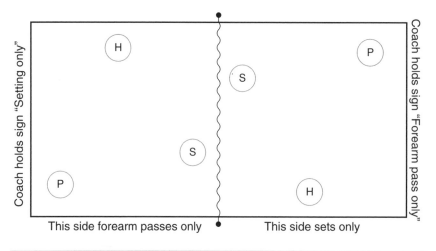

Figure 8.4 Single Skills Game.

Coaching Points. Giving visual instructions helps players learn to talk and share information on the court. Remind players that they all have a responsibility to communicate with one another.

Serving Lead-Up

Although serving is an individual skill, when a player serves in a competitive situation, team support becomes very important. Serving puts pressure on a player to get the ball into play so the team can continue performing. This unique pressure requires players to

- take time and concentrate when it's their turn to serve,
- accept that serving has an immediate impact on team spirit, and
- provide support when other servers are in the spotlight.

▬▬▬▬ Serving Lead-Up Game ▬▬▬▬

Name. Twenty-One

Purpose. To give players an opportunity to practice serves in a team-oriented and game-like situation

Organization. Use tape, rope, or hula hoops to mark targets in the locations identified in figure 8.5. Two teams of five to eight players line up on each end line facing the court. Each player has a ball. When the coach says, "Go," the first player in the serving area from each line serves. If the ball lands within a target, the server earns 3 points for his or her team. If the ball lands inside the court but outside of a target, the server earns 1 point for the team. If the player misses the serve (the ball goes into the net or out-of-bounds), no points are scored. After each two players have served, they go to the end of their respective lines and the next pair of players in line serves. The first team to score 21 points wins the game.

Coaching Points. Encourage your players to support and verbally reinforce one another when preparing to serve.

Variations. Change the location of targets so players get used to serving to different areas of the court.

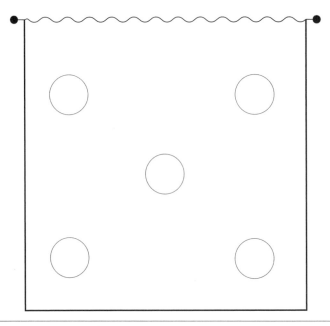

■ **Figure 8.5**   Twenty-One.

Building a Team Defense

Every time your team passes a serve or digs an attack, it is playing defense. Without good team defense (which includes digging and blocking coverage), your team will not be able to execute an effective offense. When your players know the forearm pass, teaching them team defense is mostly a matter of positioning. You want to put your players in the best position to counter whatever your opponent's offense is doing.

Being aware of the youngsters' playing tendencies can be helpful when you teach team defense. Most young attackers prefer to hit *crosscourt* rather than *down the line*. Figure 8.6 shows what crosscourt and down the line mean. For example, an opponent's left-side attacker will hit crosscourt, meaning in most cases that the left-back player will be the most likely digger of the attack. If the opponent's right-side spiker is the attacker, the right-back player will probably become the digger. To prepare your defensive positioning, therefore, you would align your diggers so they are prepared for the crosscourt attack. Young athletes will be confused as to what position they are in (crosscourt or line), and you'll want to spend ample time defining it and reminding them about these defensive concepts for positioning.

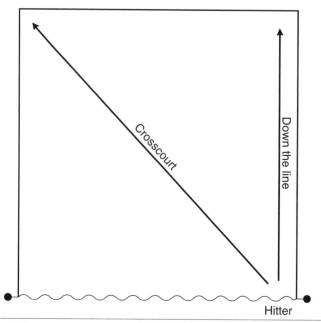

Figure 8.6 Hitting crosscourt versus hitting down the line.

Serve-Receive Considerations

The most common serve-receive alignments are the two-player serve receive and the three-player serve receive. Whichever alignment you use, many of the serves in youth volleyball tend to drop between the passers. A good rule to determine who should pass the ball is this: The passer who can *move toward the target* and pass should be the player who passes. A player who tries to receive a serve while moving away from the target will have difficulty controlling the pass and directing it to the target. In figure 8.7, for example, the passer (P) should pass the serve instead of the hitter (H): The hitter would be moving *away* from the setter (S), the target, to play the ball, whereas the passer will be moving forward and *toward* the setter.

Two-Player Serve Receive

If your opponent has a weak serving game (that is, few serves that are hard hits or difficult to pass), you can use the two-player serve receive. Many people consider passing with only two people is not

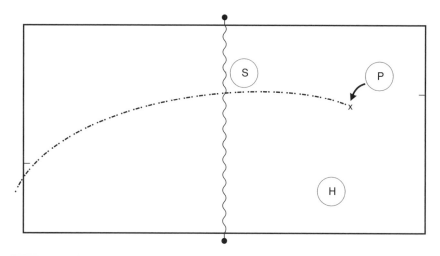

■ **Figure 8.7**   The player moving *toward* the target is the one who should pass the ball.

enough, especially with young players. The two-player serve receive, however, gives those two people responsibility for every serve that crosses the net. Passing with more than two players, on the other hand, often leads to breakdowns in communication as more people try to simultaneously communicate their decisions.

In three-on-three volleyball, two players are positioned back in the court to receive the serve (passer [P] and passer/hitter [P/H]), while the third, the setter (S), is at the net preparing to set the pass (see figure 8.8). The object for the passer and the passer/hitter is to pass the serve to the setter without causing the setter to move very far. The better the passer and the passer/hitter become at passing, the easier it will be for the setter to set a good ball for the third contact. The setter is not involved in receiving the serve in this two-player alignment. As long as the passer and the passer/hitter can handle the opposition's serves, the setter is in a very favorable court position to set and initiate the offensive attack.

Figure 8.9 illustrates the placement of a two-person serve receive in six-on-six volleyball. In most cases the left-back (LB-P) and right-back (RB-P) players will be the two youngsters receiving serves, and they will be passing to the setter (MF-S). Notice that the serve could still be played by the middle-back player (MB-C), but the emphasis will be on the left- and right-back players (LB-P and RB-P) passing the serves.

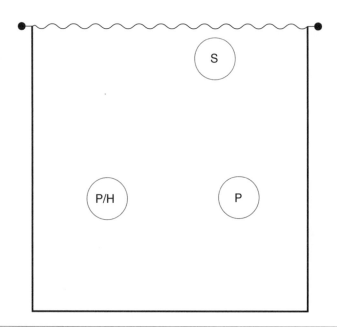

■ **Figure 8.8** Three-on-three two-player serve receive.

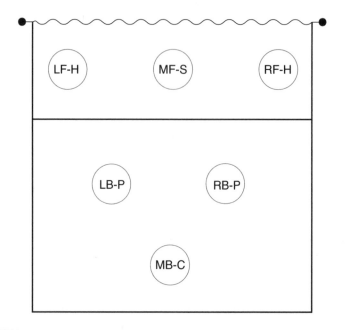

■ **Figure 8.9** Six-on-six two-player serve receive.

Three-Player Serve Receive

If your team is having difficulty receiving the serve (the ball goes erratically out of bounds or doesn't reach the setter), you can move players into a three-player serve receive. This alignment puts three players in position to receive the serve. With one more passer involved, however, communication becomes even more important. Lack of communication can quickly erase the advantages the three-player serve should provide. In most situations, the three players in the serve receive will have comparable passing ability. Sometimes, however, one passer will be slightly better. In such an instance, give this passer more responsibility, having the player pass on a greater area of the court. Just make sure the other passers are aware of this! Communication continues to be vital. Passers should always call "Ball," or "Mine," even when it might seem obvious to the player pursuing the ball. Balls that are served between two passers require still more communication. The basic rule to follow when the ball is served between two passers is this: The passer who can move into the seam *and* move in the direction of the target should take the ball. If your team members learn to both recognize this kind of situation and communicate their intentions based on the directional principle, they will succeed in the three-player serve receive.

To help decide whether to use a two-, three-, or four-person serve receive consider these circumstances. First, if you have three comparable passers, use them. To pass effectively with only two team members, you need skilled passers with above-average abilities to move and anticipate action. Second, if you are coaching beginners, brand-new to the game, opt for three players: They will get more opportunities to practice the skill of serve reception. Last, if the movement skills your players have still are not developed, choose the three-person serve receive—it will be more effective.

In three-on-three volleyball, three players can cover the court and defend the short serve (see figure 8.10a) or long serve (see figure 8.10b) more effectively. Figure 8.10a shows all three players close to the net, anticipating a short serve. The setter (S) is in position to receive a short serve in the middle, the hitter (H) at the short line, and the passer (P) at the short crosscourt angle. In figure 8.10b, the setter moves to cover the crosscourt long serve. The hitter and the passer cover the long line and the long middle-serving angles. Since the setter is the least likely to receive the long serve (this angle is the most difficult for a server to hit), he or she is in the best possible position to *set* the second ball from the hitter or the passer. If the setter receives the first contact, the passer or the hitter becomes the setter.

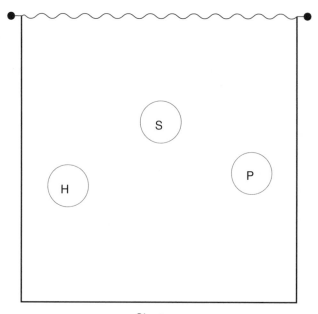

a. Short serve

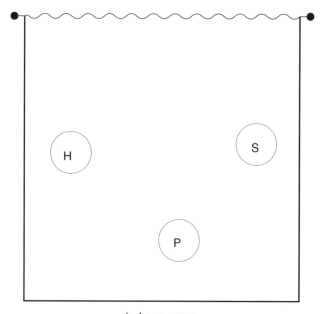

b. Long serve

■ **Figure 8.10** Three-on-three three-player serve receive of (a) a short serve and (b) a long serve.

In six-on-six volleyball, the three-player serve receive is similar to the two-person serve receive. Figure 8.11 shows that the middle-back passer (MB-P) is the third person to be incorporated into the serve receive. In serve receptions, instruct the middle-back passer to take responsibility for the deep serves.

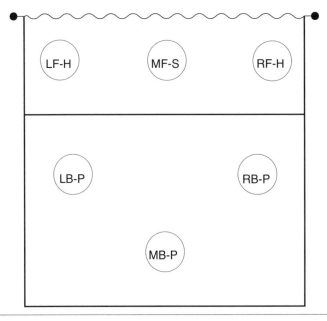

■ **Figure 8.11**   Six-on-six three-player serve receive.

Teams who pass the serve consistently keep their opponents from scoring on the serve; they also generate their own offensive attack from the good team defense.

Defensive Alignments

Some teams depend on their hitters to make aggressive attacks that score points or side outs. Others prefer to mix up their attacks by hitting hard-driven spikes combined with off-speed hits or tips. As you coach, you should watch for times when it might be wise to adjust your team's defensive alignments to fit the type of attacks the opponent is hitting. Defensively, you must decide your team's strategy based on how your players can best counter the opponent's strengths. As you now know, most attackers hit crosscourt. Unless you see opponents who can consistently hit more areas, assume that crosscourt hitting will frequently occur.

In developing your strategies, you face two basic decisions. You must decide whether to block and whether to use a free-ball alignment. Here are a few guidelines to help you decide. Before you choose to use a block, make sure you have blockers who can get their wrists over the net. Players who can't extend over the net will not be effective blockers. When you choose to incorporate a block, in effect you have decided that the opponents are capable of putting the ball down effectively. Opponents whose teams have bigger athletes or youngsters who are especially skilled as passers and hitters probably can put the ball down effectively. Moreover, choosing to block means you think you have players with the blocking ability to make significant contributions to your team's success.

Playing a defense without a block is often the better decision. If your players cannot get their wrists over the net consistently, blocking will not be effective. And opponents who do not have skilled hitters probably do not warrant a blocking defense anyway. Furthermore, if your team is especially skilled at digging, you can accentuate that ability by choosing not to block. In the end, deciding whether to block depends largely on the players you are working with: Determine what will be best for *your* team's players.

A *free-ball alignment* is best used when the *opponent* has little or no chance of putting the ball down on your defense. Free balls come over the net when the set is misdirected to the attacker or not even attacked by the offensive team, and they usually come over high and soft. A player on your opponent's team who is returning the ball with a forearm pass or set will not have a great likelihood of going to the floor on your side. The ball being returned is moving slowly and perhaps high, which gives your players ample time to move into position to play the ball. We will explain this alignment later in more detail.

Defense With a Block

Use a blocker to defend teams with a strong hitting attack. Adding blocking to your team defense will challenge opponents to either hit over or hit around the block. When blocking, either one or two players are at the net (blocking), and the other players are defending open spaces around the blocker.

Power-Spike Alignment.   When your team is playing three-on-three volleyball against a team with an aggressive (power spike) hitting attack, your blocking alignment should focus primarily on stopping the power spike from crossing the net. As illustrated in figure 8.12, the setter (S) is at the net blocking, the hitter (H) covers the short angle that is open around the block, and the passer (P) covers any ball hit down the line. Balls hit over the block (the setter) will have a high trajectory, allowing time for the passer and the hitter to communicate and cover this area.

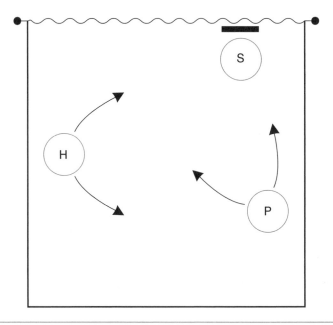

■ **Figure 8.12**   Three-on-three defensive alignment with a block against a power spike.

When your team is playing six-on-six volleyball against a team with a power-spike attack, align your players as in figure 8.13. In this alignment for a power spike coming from the opponent's left side, the middle-front (MF-B) and right-front (RF-B) players will block. The left-front (LF-D) player should be near the 10-foot line, covering any short balls off the block. Position the middle-back (MB-D) player, who will be responsible for balls hit deep or off the block, on the baseline. The left- (LB-D) and right-back (RB-D) players should be about 18 feet from the net and close to their respective sidelines; their movements will be primarily forward.

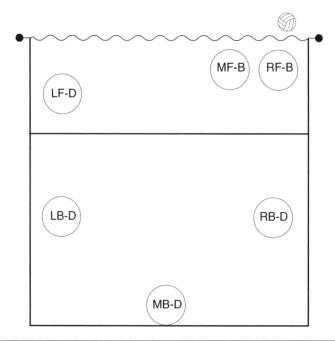

Figure 8.13 Six-on-six defensive alignment with a block against a power spike.

Off-Speed Hit Alignment. Opponents who "read" (see) your block may use an off-speed hit to avoid it. An off-speed hit will not have maximal force, as it's a soft hit placed to a part of the court with no defenders. The defensive alignment to use against the off-speed hit puts your players in position to dig this attack effectively. In three-on-three volleyball, you would position the setter (S) at the net to attempt to block or deflect any type of offensive attack. The passer (P) moves in to cover the off-speed hit or tip just behind the setter's block. The hitter (H) covers the backcourt area for any long off-speed hits or tips (see figure 8.14). Communication is essential in this type of defense. Who will play the ball depends largely on where it is placed and who has the best angle to make the play. Watching the attacker is usually the best way for the defense to know what to do. Players who have slow approaches or who have been blocked consistently will look to tip or off-speed hits in hopes of scoring points or side outs. While the off-speed attack can be used as an effective offensive weapon, it more typically is used when attackers lack confidence that they can attack the ball around the block.

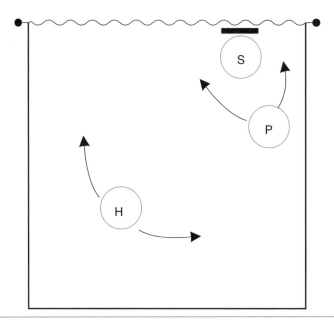

Figure 8.14 Three-on-three defensive alignment with a block against an off-speed hit.

In six-on-six volleyball, the off-speed hit alignment is essentially the same as the power-spike alignment. The only difference between them is the position of the left-front digger (LF-D). This player should assume more responsibility for digging the off-speed attack, since these attacks primarily are directed to the middle of the court (see figure 8.15). Recognizing the off-speed attack is critical to defending against it! An opponent's attacker who approaches slowly or whose arm swings slowly is likely to hit an off-speed shot. Players who have consistently been blocked also are likely to try an off-speed attack to avoid getting blocked again. Encourage your players to pursue the off-speed attack on their feet and to try to stay off the ground.

Defense Without a Block

Suppose you have decided, either because your players can't get their wrists over the net or because your opponents are hitting a lot of free balls, that you do not need to use a block in your team defense. You have made a good decision, but now you must consider

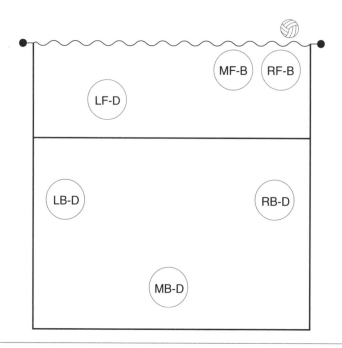

■ **Figure 8.15** Six-on-six defensive alignment with a block against an off-speed hit.

just where to position your players to defend against the attackers who, after all, do not have to hit around your block. Remembering that the attackers tend to hit crosscourt, even if there is no block up, will help you determine where to place your defenders.

There are three different alignments you will need to teach your players when they're playing without a block: the free-ball alignment, power-spike alignment, and off-speed hit alignment. These alignments correspond to and prepare your players to defend against the three varieties of offensive attacks.

Free-Ball Alignment. Free balls are usually hit high, soft, and deep. A block will not be effective in defending a free-ball attack. In three-on-three volleyball with no block, all three players are free to help pass the ball. The hitter (H) moves back to cover the crosscourt angle (see figure 8.16). The passer (P) covers the middle of the court, and the setter (S) backs off the net awaiting the pass from either the hitter or the passer to start the offensive attack. On a high, soft free ball, the hitter and the passer should have sufficient time to get to the ball and make the defensive dig.

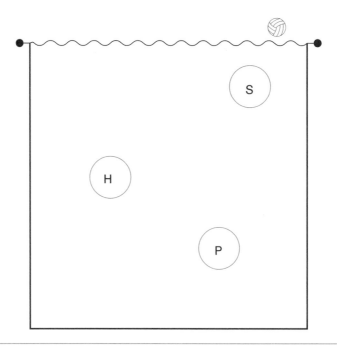

Figure 8.16 Three-on-three free-ball defensive alignment.

Error Detection and Correction for Defensive Alignments

When should a team block? How does a coach know when to change the team's serve-receive and defensive alignment?

ERROR: Players are frustrated in trying to dig a strong attack. The blocker is not effective in slowing down or altering the attack. Your nonblocking players are struggling to dig balls hit to them, and you can't seem to stop your opponent's offense.

CORRECTION
1. Change to a three-player serve receive and free-ball defensive alignment. This will put three players into position instead of two for the pass or dig.
2. If your team has not thoroughly developed its blocking fundamentals, the three-person alignment gives players the best opportunity to cover the court defensively.

For six-on-six volleyball, you'll deploy your players in more of a spread arrangement for a free-ball alignment (see figure 8.17). Instruct your left-front (LF-P/H) and right-front (RF-P/H) players to pull off, or back from, the net to the 10-foot line to play any free ball that starts to land in front of them. If the middle-front (MF-S) player is the setter, instruct the LF-P/H and RF-P/H players to stay on the net so that they can set the second ball. Any ball going deeper into their court should be played by the backcourt players; they will balance the court, each being responsible for one-third of the area.

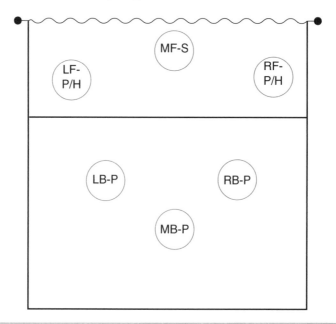

■ **Figure 8.17** Six-on-six free-ball defensive alignment.

Power-Spike Alignment. If your team is defending a power spike without a blocker in three-on-three volleyball, move your players back off the net in position to cover the angles of the court. The hitter (H) will cover the crosscourt angle, the setter (S) the attack down the line, and the passer (P) the area between these two angles (see figure 8.18). All three players should be in ready position to dig a hard-driven spike.

With six players, the placement of the back row in a power-spike alignment is about the same without a blocker as with one (see figure 8.19). A primary difference between these blocking situations, however, is the flexibility your defenders should have. Without a block, the back row players need more freedom in making movements they

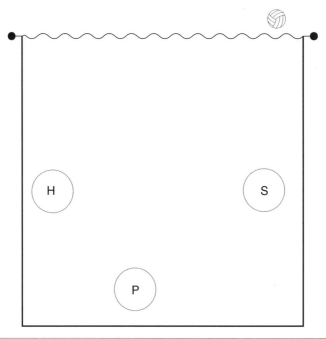

■ **Figure 8.18**   Three-on-three power-spike defensive alignment without a block.

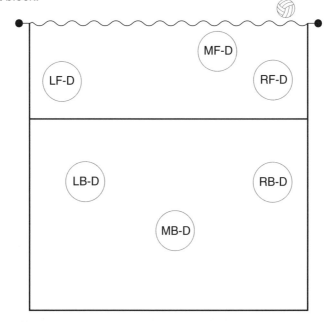

■ **Figure 8.19**   Six-on-six power-spike defensive alignment without a block.

think will effectively dig the opponent's attack. Be sure to set parameters for each back-row defender, however, so no confusion arises between defenders as to who should dig a particular ball.

The placement of the front row also becomes important to consider, since these players will not be blocking. In figure 8.19, notice that the two front-row players closer to the point of attack (MF-D and RF-D) will pull off the net 5 to 6 feet to defend against off-speed attacks. The blocker farthest from the point of attack (LF-D) in essence becomes a back-row defender. Having the middle- and right-front players responsible for off-speed attacks frees the back-row defenders to concentrate on any hard-driven spikes that go deep into their court.

Off-Speed Hit Alignment. To defend an off-speed hit or tip without a blocker at the net, players move in closer to the net to pick up short, soft hits. With three players, the hitter (H) covers the crosscourt angle, the setter (S) covers the short court (near the net), and the passer (P) plays the deep court (see figure 8.20).

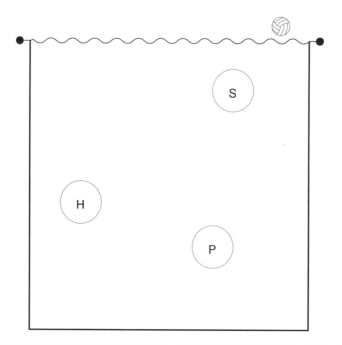

■ **Figure 8.20**   Three-on-three off-speed defensive alignment without a block.

Opponents sometimes use the off-speed hit to throw the defensive team off balance. Remind your players to talk and call for the ball in making the first dig. In six-on-six volleyball, the off-speed and power-spike alignments are similar except that the left-front digger (LF-D) comes in 3 to 4 feet from the sideline (see figure 8.21). A good front row can see and dig the off-speed attack, and this is what you should hope to help your young players learn. Encourage the back-row defenders to take responsibility for any off-speed attacks that fall between the front and back rows. A digger who is moving forward toward the ball has a better chance at making a well-placed dig.

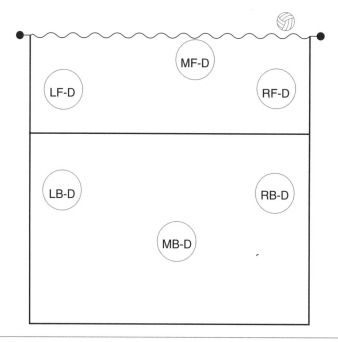

■ **Figure 8.21** Six-on-six off-speed hit defensive alignment without a block.

Offensive and Defensive Transition

How quick and balanced your team is as it moves between defense and offense is called *transition*. Preparing your team to execute offensively and defensively is part of good strategy; training your players to make effective transitions will enhance their success still further. Figure 8.22 illustrates how a transition in three-on-three volleyball might work. This sequence applies as well to two-, four-, and six-player volleyball teams. The ball is put in play with the serve (1). The opposing team must pass the serve (2), set (3), and attack (4) offensively. The defensive team may block (5) and/or dig (6) the attack and then begin its offense. Playing the team's defense (blocking and digging) and controlling the serve or offensive attack all start the transition to team offense. *Recovery* is the key word in describing volleyball transitions. The quicker a team can recover from an opponent's attack and reassure its control of the ball, the quicker it can set up its offensive attack.

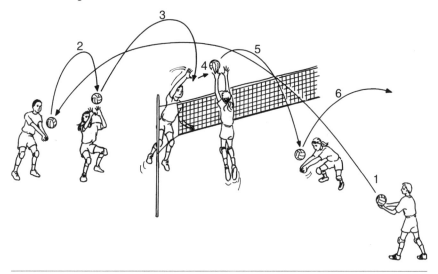

■ **Figure 8.22** Offensive and defensive transition.

Developing a quick recovery in transition helps players adjust to a variety of attacks (the power spike, off-speed, or free ball), and the participants learn how to move from the pass into offensive patterns. Teach the concept of transition as you review the serve-receive and defensive alignments in the following drills.

Transition Drills

Name. Transition Recognition Drill

Purpose. To teach players how to react to different offensive attacks and execute the proper defense

Organization.   Divide the group into several three-player teams. Set the first team in a two- or three-player serve-receive alignment (see "Serve-Receive Considerations" earlier in this unit). After aligning the players, toss or hit the ball over the net. Teams must pass the toss or serve (play defense) and move to set and attack the ball (transition into team offense). According to your players' abilities and ages, you can begin calling out various defensive alignments as they move to defend the attack. For example, you might yell "Free ball" or "Power spike with one blocker." The players quickly move to their proper defensive positions and attempt to defend the coach's serve or attack. Keep score by awarding a point for a proper alignment and a point for each contact (three contacts maximum for each side). Once your players get comfortable with this drill, add players to incorporate appropriate movements for six on six. Trying to do this drill right away with six on six will cause you and your players confusion—start with three on three!

Coaching Points.   Initially, the coach will need to help each team set up for the different alignments and will have to answer questions. Your players will be much better off if you take the time to help them understand why they are moving to different positions for each situation. As their understanding develops, move the drill along quickly and insist that each team hustle into the court and listen for its defensive alignment.

Name.   Champs of the Court Drill

Purpose.   To help teams adjust to different offensive attacks and practice their defensive-to-offensive transition patterns

Organization.   Divide players into two-, three-, four-, or six-player teams and start with two teams on the court on opposite sides of the net (see figure 8.23). The champs' side serves, and the other sets up in serve-receive alignment (two or three players). The volley is played out; the team that wins the volley obtains the serve and stays on the court. The team that didn't score leaves the court, and it is replaced by another three-player team. Points may be scored only by the team on the point side of the court. If the challenging team wins the next volley, it moves to the point side (the champs' side) of the court and gets a point for every volley it wins. Teams rotate off and wait for their next turn to play. Play to 15 points.

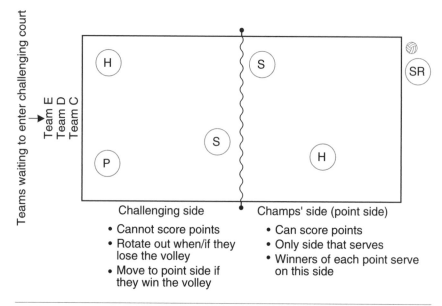

Teams waiting to enter challenging court

→ Team E
Team D
Team C

Challenging side
- Cannot score points
- Rotate out when/if they lose the volley
- Move to point side if they win the volley

Champs' side (point side)
- Can score points
- Only side that serves
- Winners of each point serve on this side

■ **Figure 8.23** Champs of the Court Drill.

Coaching Points. Teams struggling with serve receive can change from a two-player to a three-player alignment. In a game situation, a coach would make this decision. In this drill, the players learn to communicate and make decisions about team play on their own.

Putting It All Together

This guide has introduced you to an innovative and refreshing approach to volleyball for beginning players. The skills, drills, and strategies you've read about are relatively simple and readily taught to eager learners.

We hope that you, too, will be an eager learner. As you gain experience in coaching, keep your players' welfare as your top priority. Be upbeat, keep things fun, and be patient. A good teacher and coach does all these things. Your new role has many responsibilities, but we're confident that after reading *Coaching Youth Volleyball*, you're well on your way to becoming a good coach!

Take the Next Step!

The Coaching Accreditation Program (CAP) represents an educational commitment by USA Volleyball, volleyball's national governing body. CAP provides on-going education for coaches in an effort to advance the sport of volleyball. Coaches create valuable experiences for all those people who enjoy volleyball. USA Volleyball wants to thank you for volunteering to coach your volleyball team and for caring enough to learn how to be a better coach.

This next step is *yours:* Consider the CAP program, which is designed to unravel some of the mysteries you will encounter daily as a volleyball coach. You can easily learn the answers to many of these mysteries from this book—and everything in this book works! A highly recommended complement to *Coaching Youth Volleyball* is available in USA Volleyball's *IMPACT Manual.* It provides you with material on volleyball resources, drill development, and the many other resources that USA Volleyball has to offer you. As you do more coaching and receive the rewards that come with it, you will want to know even more to help you comfortably handle the new situations coming your way. This is why USA Volleyball created CAP.

CAP courses are offered throughout the country year-round. Level I and II courses are step-by-step, in-depth opportunities to learn skill training and game strategies. Following each course, coaches complete additional home study and testing. Personal feedback is an important ingredient of our learning process. With perseverance and study, everyone succeeds!

Finishing the CAP process extends more volleyball benefits to you. Contemporary coaching concepts and ideas from CAP publications and resources keep you up to date on this dynamic game. In addition, CAP involvement can introduce you to the myriad of multimedia resources available through Volleyball Informational Products (VIP), a joint venture between USA Volleyball and the American Volleyball Coaches Association. VIP provides a number of excellent publications and videos that aid you in your efforts to become the most knowledgeable and skilled coach possible.

Ultimately, the CAP program helps you expand your expertise and experience as a coach. Coaching your volleyball team with confidence will help you meet the challenges of this great, universal game. The players will be eager to have you as their coach!

To learn more about the next step for *you*, please write or call

USA Volleyball
Educational Development
3595 E. Fountain Blvd., Suite I-2
Colorado Springs, CO 80910-1740
(800) 275-8782

Appendix A

Organizations to Contact for Coaching Children With Disabilities

American Athletic Association of the Deaf
3607 Washington Boulevard, Suite 4
Ogden, UT 84403-1737
(801) 393-8710
TTY: (801) 393-7916
Fax: (801) 393-2263

Disabled Sports USA
451 Hungerford Drive, Suite 100
Rockville, MD 20850
(301) 217-0960

Paralyzed Veterans of America
801 18th Street NW
Washington, DC 20006
(202) 872-1300
(800) 424-8200

Special Olympics International
1325 G Street NW, Suite 500
Washington, DC 20005
(202) 628-3630

U.S. Association of Blind Athletes
33 North Institute
Colorado Springs, CO 80903
(719) 630-0422

U.S. Cerebral Palsy Athletic Association
3810 West NW Highway, Suite 205
Dallas, TX 75220
(214) 351-1510

U.S. Les Autres Sports Association
1475 West Gray, Suite 166
Houston, TX 77019-4926
(713) 521-3737

Appendix B

Sample Season Plan for Beginning Volleyball Players

Goal: To help players learn and practice the individual skills and team tactics needed to play volleyball games successfully.

T(#) = Initial skill teaching time (minutes)
P(#) = Review and practice time (minutes)
* = Skills practiced during drills and activities

Skills	Week 1		Week 2		Week 3		Week 4	
	Day 1	Day 2	Day 1	Day 2	Day 1	Day 2	Day 1	Day 2
Warm-Up	T(10)	P(5)	P(5)	P(5)	P(5)	P(5)	P(5)	P(5)
Cool-Down	T(5)	P(5)	P(5)	P(5)	P(5)	P(5)	P(5)	P(5)
General rules	T(5)							
Violations	T(5)	P(5)						
Evaluation	(5)	(5)	(5)	(5)	(5)	(5)	(5)	(5)
Serving								
Underhand	T(5)	P(5)	*	*	*	*	*	*
Overhand		T(5)	*	*	*	*	*	*
Drills	T(10)	P(10)	P(10)	P(5)	P(5)	P(5)	P(5)	
Forearm passing								
Body position	T(5)	*	*	*	*	*	*	*
Serve receive		T(5)	*	P(5)	*	*	*	*
Drills	T(10)	P(10)	P(10)	P(5)	P(5)	P(5)	P(10)	

Skills (*continued*)	Week 1 Day 1	Week 1 Day 2	Week 2 Day 1	Week 2 Day 2	Week 3 Day 1	Week 3 Day 2	Week 4 Day 1	Week 4 Day 2
Overhand passing								
Body position	T(5)	*			*	*	*	*
Setting		T(10)	P(10)	*	*	*	*	*
Attack								
Armswing			T(5)	*	*		*	*
Footwork and jumping				T(5)		*	*	*
Drills			T(5)	P(10)	P(10)	P(5)		P(5)
Blocking								
Body position			T(5)	*	*	*	*	
Reading attack				T(5)	*	*		*
Drills			T(5)	P(5)	P(5)	P(5)		P(5)
Team offense								
Player positions				T(5)	*	*	*	*
Alignments				T(5)	P(5)	*	*	*
Drills					T(10)	P(10)	P(10)	P(5)
Team defense								
Player positions					T(10)	P(5)	*	*
Alignments						T(5)	*	*
Drills					T(10)	T(10)	P(10)	P(10)
Lead-up games						T(5)	P(10)	
Scrimmage*							T(15)	P(30)

*Three-on-three scrimmages are excellent starting points, regardless of whether your team will be playing 3 on 3, 4 on 4, or 6 on 6. Three-on-three volleyball gives players more opportunities to touch the ball.

Appendix C

Commonly Used Volleyball Officiating Signals

Side out

Ball in bounds
or line violation

Ball out

Ball contacted by
a player and going
out-of-bounds

Four hits

Crossing
center line

Held ball, thrown ball,
lifted ball, or carried ball

Double hit

Ball contacted
below the waist

Substitution

Ball served into net or
player touching net

Over the net

Double fault
or play over

Illegal block
or screen

Point

ASEP Volunteer Level

The American Sport Education Program (ASEP) offers three Volunteer Level curriculums for adults who work with youth sport:

■ SportCoach   ■ SportParent   ■ SportDirector

SportCoach

ASEP's SportCoach Program consists of two courses:

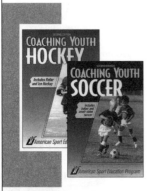

The **Rookie Coaches Course** provides inexperienced coaches with essential information for teaching the skills and strategies of a sport, including sample practice plans. Companion coaching guides are available for baseball, basketball, football, gymnastics, hockey, ski racing, softball, soccer, swimming, tennis, volleyball, and wrestling.

The **Coaching Young Athletes Course** is for second-year coaches and others who want more instruction in the principles of coaching than is offered in the Rookie Course.

SportParent

ASEP's SportParent Course is a 1- to 2-hour program that provides youth sport administrators and coaches with a practical and effective way to educate parents about their children's participation in sports.

The SportParent Course Package includes the *SportParent Facilitator Manual,* the *SportParent Video,* the *SportParent Survival Guide,* and the *SportParent* book.

SportDirector

ASEP's SportDirector Program offers outstanding opportunities for youth sport directors to improve sport programs for the children in their community. The program includes a very practical *Youth SportDirector Guide* and a dynamic workshop.

American Sport Education Program

P.O. Box 5076
Champaign, IL 61825-5076
Fax: 217-351-1549

**For more information
on ASEP's Volunteer Level
programs, call Toll-Free
1-800-747-5698.**

More Volleyball Books
─ From HK ─

Mike Hebert
1991 • Cloth • 224 pp • Item PHEB0423
ISBN 0-88011-423-1
$23.00 ($31.95 Canadian)

**William J. Neville, USA Volleyball
(formerly US Volleyball Association)**
1990 • Paper • 224 pp • Item PNEV0362
ISBN 0-88011-362-6 • $19.95 ($29.95 Canadian)

(Second Edition)

**Barbara L. Viera and
Bonnie Jill Ferguson**
1996 • Paper • 168 pp • Item PVIE0646
ISBN 0-87322-646-1 • $15.95 ($22.95 Canadian)

Carl McGown, Editor
1994 • Paper • 184 pp • Item PMCG0572
ISBN 0-87322-572-4
$14.95 ($21.95 Canadian)

To place your book order, U.S. customers call **TOLL FREE 1-800-747-4457**.
Customers outside the U.S. place your order using the appropriate telephone
number/address shown in the front of this book.

HUMAN KINETICS
The Premier Publisher for Sports & Fitness
www.humankinetics.com